Praise for *Promote Your Purpose*

"So many authors pour their hearts into writing a book only to hit a wall when it comes to marketing; they're unsure where to start, what to do, or even what they don't yet know. Jenn's book changes all of that. It's like having a multiple-award-winning author and publisher right in your pocket, offering advice that's as punchy as it is practical. With her signature mix of expertise and encouragement, Jenn helps you build the right foundation before you take action, grounding every tactic in the mindset and perspective you need to actually succeed. This isn't just another marketing manual. It's a trusted guide for every author who wants their book to truly reach readers."

— A. Y. Berthiaume
CEO of The Write Place, Right Time
Award-Winning Coauthor of *Do Not Write a Book . . . Until You Read This One*

"*Promote Your Purpose* is the essential guide every purpose-driven author needs once the publishing dust settles. It transforms book marketing from something overwhelming into a clear, strategic, and heartfelt process. The ASPEN Method framework provides structure while honoring each author's unique vision. This book does more than teach marketing—it redefines it as an act of service that helps authors build authentic connections and expand their impact with clarity and confidence."

— Susan Friedmann, CSP
International Bestselling Author of *Riches in Niches:
How to Make it BIG in a Small Market*

"Jenn T. Grace makes marketing feel deeply human. She writes with honesty and empathy and a clarity that turns strategy into something meaningful, anchoring the entire book in her ASPEN Method: a simple, proven framework that takes the guesswork out of promoting your work. Through her guidance, I learned that promoting your work doesn't have to mean compromising your values; it can be an extension of your purpose. This book reminded me that visibility can be an act of generosity."

— Nell Derick Debevoise Dewey
Author, Speaker, EQUUS Facilitator, Creator of Lead in 3D

"In *Promote Your Purpose*, Jenn T. Grace provides clarity in what can often feel like a confusing and chaotic process: how to market your book. Her ASPEN Method framework creates a methodology any author can use to determine how to most strategically position their book for their specific reader and let the rest of it go. Jenn blends business strategy with a human-centered approach, showing how to build a platform rooted in values and service, and her methods have personally helped me stay laser-focused on how to get the most out of my book so I can have the biggest impact with my audience. This book gave me language for something I'd always felt but couldn't quite articulate—that my work has impact when it's grounded in purpose. I no longer think of marketing as "selling." I see it as a way to connect with the people who truly need what I offer. I cannot recommend Jenn's work more highly!"

— Michelle Feferman
CEO and Founder of Equity at Work
Author of *Do DEI Right*

"What sets this book apart is how Jenn balances practicality with purpose. She acknowledges and nurtures the impact we want to make in the world, all the while ensuring every concept builds toward real-world application, not theory. I haven't even written my book yet, but having this field guide to what comes after I do so has taken a huge weight off my shoulders. There are so many peers of mine I'll be gifting this book to, including brilliant thought leaders who write their books and struggle to market them afterward. This book is going to be the missing link for a lot of underrecognized authors."

— N. Chloé Nwangwu
The Brand Scientist™
Speaker and Principal Investigator at NobiWorks

"Jenn provides an incredible depth of marketing insight that I haven't found anywhere else. Before discovering her work, I searched for clear, accessible guidance for authors and found only expensive, unclear options tied to publishing contracts. Jenn's approach is completely different. It's transparent, strategic, and full of practical tools and trade secrets that have helped me truly understand what's involved in marketing a book. The information is super organized, full of examples, and leaves me feeling both empowered and inspired to keep building momentum. Marketing is absolutely Jenn's superpower, and I'm grateful for how generously she shares her expertise."

— Christiane Scarpino
Speaker, Advocate for PTSD Awareness
Author of *Missing Pieces*

"I consider myself a reluctant marketer—hesitant and sometimes nervous to put myself out there—and I'm also not very sophisticated about marketing tools and techniques. So for me, *Promote Your Purpose* is a lifeline and a goldmine. Jenn's entire approach keeps me centered on why I'm trying to get the word out about my book, which is to serve my clients and readers with my message and strategies, not to sell books or myself. From this foundation, I can choose what feels authentic and empowering from the wealth of practical strategies, ideas, and tools that fill these pages (and her online resources, too). I know that I will come back to *Promote Your Purpose* again and again to get a shot of Jenn's encouraging tone, to find fresh ideas, and to keep moving forward toward a larger and more meaningful impact in the world."

— Cathy Alfandre
Career Coach
Author of *Breaking Free from a Malignant Manager*

PROMOTE YOUR PURPOSE

PROMOTE YOUR PURPOSE

A Strategic Guide to Book Marketing for Nonfiction Authors Who Want to Grow Their Impact, Influence, and Income

JENN T. GRACE

Copyright (C) 2026 Jenn T. Grace. All rights reserved.

No part of this publication shall be reproduced, transmitted, or sold in whole or in part in any form without prior written consent of the author, except as provided by the United States of America copyright law. Any unauthorized usage of the text without express written permission of the publisher is a violation of the author's copyright and is illegal and punishable by law. All trademarks and registered trademarks appearing in this guide are the property of their respective owners.

For permission requests, write to the publisher, addressed "Attention: Permissions Coordinator," at the address below.

Publish Your Purpose
141 Weston Street, #155
Hartford, CT, 06141

The opinions expressed by the author are not necessarily those held by Publish Your Purpose.

Ordering information: Quantity sales and special discounts are available on quantity purchases by corporations, associations, and others. For details, contact the publisher at hello@publishyourpurpose.com.

Edited by: Nancy Graham-Tillman
Cover design by: Mark Pate
Typeset by: Nelly Murariu

Printed in the United States of America.
ISBN: 979-8-88797-211-4 (hardcover)
ISBN: 979-8-88797-212-1 (Ingram paperback)
ISBN: 979-8-88797-217-6 (KDP paperback)
ISBN: 979-8-88797-213-8 (ebook)

Library of Congress Control Number: 2026900397

First edition, April 2026. 1.1

The information contained within this book is strictly for informational purposes. The material may include information, products, or services by third parties. As such, the Author and Publisher do not assume responsibility or liability for any third-party material or opinions. The publisher is not responsible for websites (or their content) that are not owned by the publisher. Readers are advised to do their own due diligence when it comes to making decisions.

Publish Your Purpose is a hybrid publisher of nonfiction books. Our mission is to elevate the voices often excluded from traditional publishing. We intentionally seek out authors and storytellers with diverse backgrounds, life experiences, and unique perspectives to publish books that will make an impact in the world. Do you have a book idea you would like us to consider publishing? Please visit PublishYourPurpose.com for more information.

DEDICATION

To the authors who believed in their stories—and in us.
Thank you for teaching us that writing, publishing, and
promoting a book is never just about the book
but also about the changes you create along the way.
Your stories have fed my insatiable appetite for
knowledge, growth, and connection. Without you,
there would be no books—and no Publish Your Purpose.

RETHINKING LEADERSHIP IN THE AGE OF AI

This book intentionally does not cover AI. The systems' capabilities and impact are evolving too rapidly for any printed book to keep up, but that doesn't mean it's not reshaping how we lead, communicate, and market our work. In fact, it's already transforming the way books are promoted, thought leadership is expressed, and audiences are reached. Rather than offer static insights, I, alongside my friend and colleague Jennifer Brown, created a living, evolving resource to explore how AI intersects with purpose-driven leadership. Together we're navigating the human side of AI and cocreating new ways of showing up, sharing stories, and leading with intention.

To view our resource please visit:
promoteyourpurposebook.com/bonuses.

CONTENTS

Preface — xvii
Introduction — xxv

PART 1: BUILDING YOUR FOUNDATION — 1

1. Clarify Your Purpose, Vision, and Impact — 3
2. Set Strategic Goals That Drive Real Change — 15
3. Build a Marketing Mindset That Fuels Growth — 37
4. Stay Motivated with Support, Structure, and Accountability — 53
5. Turn Your Book Into an Ecosystem — 65
6. Know Your Reader, Know Your Buyer, Know Your Impact — 81
7. Sell with Purpose, Serve with Confidence — 95

PART 2: THE ASPEN METHOD — 111

8. Assess Your Platform, Purpose, and Possibilities — 115
9. Strategize Your Visibility and Audience Growth — 139
10. Plan and Promote Your Book with Intention — 167
11. Execute Consistently and Create Momentum — 199
12. Nurture Your Book's Impact for Years to Come — 227

Conclusion   Your Next Chapter Starts Now — 253

APPENDICES 259

A: Your Book Marketing Essentials Checklist 261
B: TEDx and Signature Talks (Ch. 2) 267
C: Calls to Action Examples (Ch. 10) 275
D: Key Ad Metrics for Paid Campaigns (Ch. 11) 279
E: Marketing to Academic Institutions (Ch. 11) 283
F: Your On-the-Go Author Kit (Ch. 11) 287
G: Book Launch Email Examples (Ch. 11) 289

Reader Resources 295
Acknowledgments 297
About Jenn 299
Other Books By The Author 300
Hire Jenn to Speak 301
The B Corp Movement 302

ASK ME ABOUT MY BOOK

Want a free "Ask Me About My Book" sticker? It's a great way to spark curiosity and draw attention to yourself as an author in a subtle, approachable way. Stick it on your laptop, water bottle, or notebook to invite conversation wherever you go. Just submit your receipt for this book through the contact form at promoteyourpurposebook.com/sticker, and I'll mail one to you!

ASK ME ABOUT MY BOOK

PREFACE

Dear Reader,

Hi there! Welcome to *Promote Your Purpose*. My name is Jenn, and I'm here to help you turn your message into momentum.

Whether you've just published your first book or you're considering how to amplify the impact of a previous one, this book is here to help you transform your work into a tool for thought leadership and meaningful change.

Back in 2012, I didn't know where to start with publishing or promoting my book. But as a consultant working in the financial services and insurance industries, I kept hearing the same questions from clients and conference planners:

- "Jenn, when are you going to write a book?"
- "Do you have a book I can read to get a sense of your approach?"

At the time, I wasn't sure if I could do it, or whether anyone would care. As a child I dreamed of being a Dear Abby–style advice columnist, so writing wasn't the challenge. But a book? That felt so much bigger than penning advice columns. It was a daunting leap. Yet the more I heard those questions, the more I realized how important a book could be, not just as a personal achievement but as a way to expand my influence, solidify my credibility, and grow my business.

That realization was my first wake-up call, but the real transformation happened when I took the leap to publish my first book in 2013.

Books as Catalysts for Change

My first book was far from perfect. I was proud to have achieved such a big milestone, but I quickly realized how much I didn't know about publishing. I made mistakes, including not fully understanding the importance of editing or how to position the book effectively for my audience.

Even though it wasn't everything I hoped it would be, that first book still opened doors, started conversations, and helped me reach people I might never have connected with otherwise. By the time I published my second book a year later, I'd learned from those early mistakes. I approached the process with more confidence, better preparation, and a clearer strategy, and this time the results were different. The book gained traction, built momentum, and elevated my visibility.

The lesson was clear: A book doesn't need to be perfect to make an impact, but it does need to be professional. A polished, well-edited, and thoughtfully presented book builds trust in the author, reflects their credibility, and boosts their reputation as a thought leader, which ensures their message is taken seriously and resonates with the audience they're striving to impact. And when that book demonstrates care, it strengthens that connection and builds confidence in an author's expertise.

As for me, it soon became even more apparent that this professionalism wasn't just enhancing my ability to share my message but was elevating how others saw me. My books weren't just tools for communicating ideas; they became powerful assets that positioned me as a thought leader in my field.

The journey from my first to my second book taught me the value of learning from experience and sharing that knowledge. As I gained confidence, I realized I could guide others through their own journeys, helping them avoid common pitfalls and amplify their messages. I started sharing my publishing experiences with others, and I hosted coffee chats, answered questions, and mentored friends who were navigating their own publishing journeys. What started as casual conversations quickly became something bigger: *What if I could help others use books to promote their purpose, elevate their voices, and create real change?*

Helping Others Find Their Paths

I never set out to start a publishing company. It found me.

In early 2015, I was part of an entrepreneurial group coaching program, and someone casually asked, "Jenn, what if you helped other people write and publish their books?" By then I had already self-published three books, and people in my network were frequently reaching out to "pick my brain" about the process. I shared coffee after coffee, explaining what I'd learned, the mistakes I'd made, and what I'd do differently, and soon I brought up the idea in the coaching group: "You know, I've been thinking about teaching others how to publish their books. Do you think there's something there?"

My coach immediately said, "Yes! But sell it before you create it."

That was some of the best advice I've ever received.

So, in February 2016, I approached seven people in my network who I knew wanted to write a book, and I told them, "I don't have a program built yet, but I know how to guide you through this process. If you're not one hundred percent satisfied, I'll give you your money back."

To my surprise, all seven said yes.

Over the next three months, I worked with those authors to test and refine a system, which eventually became a flagship writing program. By the end of the year, I had run the program three more times, making improvements with each round. But something happened during that process that changed everything. One of the participants, a talented and passionate aspiring author, pulled me aside after class and said, "Jenn, I think you need to start a publishing company."

At first I dismissed the idea. I didn't know how to start or run a publishing company. I'd figured out how to publish my own books and teach others how to do it, but launching a full-fledged publishing company to bring other people's books to life? That felt like a whole new level.

Yet the idea stuck with me.

I sat with this only through the weekend before I realized, *This is what I'm meant to do.* I knew firsthand how transformative it was to see my words in print, to hold my book in my hands, and to share my message with an audience. And I wanted to help others experience that transformation too, especially those who might not otherwise have the opportunity.

In August 2016, Publish Your Purpose (PYP) officially launched. Eight months after that seed was planted, we published our first book, and by the end of our first year we had published 12 books, each one amplifying the voice of an author with an important story to tell. At the time of writing *this* book, we've published over 200 books.

But the journey hasn't been without challenges, and one early failure taught me a vital lesson.

Not About Perfection

For over two decades, I've honed my marketing skills in both practice and education, helping brands and authors craft their messages, connect with audiences, and drive meaningful engagement. But none of this would've happened if I'd let my past failures define me. And though my background in marketing and communications provides the tools I need to help authors craft compelling messages and connect with audiences, I failed my first marketing class when I was an undergrad. At the time it felt devastating, and I questioned whether I was cut out for the field at all. But I didn't give up. I pushed forward, worked harder, and eventually earned a master's degree in integrated marketing communications. This full-circle moment taught me that your failures don't define you.

This is the same message I now share with every author I work with. Many feel daunted by the idea of marketing their book, worrying they're "not good at it" or that they don't have the skills. But I'm here to tell you this: You do not have to be perfect, and you do not have to get it right on the first try. What matters is showing up, having a willingness to learn, and staying committed to your purpose.

At PYP, we've built a process that takes the fear and guesswork out of marketing so you can focus on what truly matters: sharing your story, connecting with your audience, and making an impact. We're here to guide you every step of the way, whether you're standing in front of a crowd of 500 or quietly writing your next chapter.

That's the heart of PYP. It's not just about publishing books; it's about creating opportunities—for you, for your audience, and for the world we're all striving to make better.

What This Book Is About

From the beginning, PYP has been about amplifying voices, empowering communities, and creating a ripple effect of positive change. Many authors we work with are experts in their fields and write about topics they're deeply passionate about or their lived experiences. Their stories are powerful, their messages are urgent, and the world needs to hear them. This is why marketing is not an afterthought in this book, nor should it be with yours. Marketing is at the heart of your next chapter.

Promote Your Purpose is not about how to write or publish a book but about what comes next. If you're just starting your writing or publishing journey, my first book, *Publish Your Purpose: A Step-By-Step Guide to Write, Publish, and Grow Your Big Idea*, provides guidance on bringing your book to life. This book, however, is about leveraging your book to amplify your impact, influence, and income.

There's no single roadmap to success. What resonates deeply with one author might feel completely off-base for another, and that's by design. The goal is to help you find strategies that feel authentic to you. And for many authors, especially those from underrecognized communities, self-publishing is the *only* viable route to sharing their stories, yet the industry still treats "traditional publishing" as the gold standard and controls access to major distribution, media coverage, and awards. *Promote Your Purpose* was written with that imbalance in mind. Throughout, you'll find strategies that help self-published, independent, and hybrid authors build the same credibility, visibility, and revenue opportunities that gatekeepers have long reserved for traditionally published books.

So, this book is for thought leaders, aspiring changemakers, and anyone who wants to use their book as a catalyst for impact. Your book is more than a product. It's a platform. It's a way to amplify your voice, establish your credibility, and connect with your audience in a meaningful way.

If even the word *marketing* feels uncomfortable, you're not alone (I failed my first marketing class, after all). But marketing, when done right, is not about selling. It's about serving. Using a simple and proven method, you'll discover how to take actionable steps to align your marketing with your purpose. Whether your goal is to book more speaking engagements, grow your business, or inspire your readers, this method will help you get there.

Remember: Marketing isn't just about selling books. It's about building a legacy that reflects your impact.

Remember: Marketing isn't just about selling books. It's about building a legacy that reflects your impact.

You Are Good Enough

If you've ever doubted yourself, you're not alone. Many authors ask themselves questions like these:

- "Who am I to really sell my book? Who actually cares?"
- "My book is already out there, and I don't know where to start with marketing."
- "I'm not a natural salesperson. How do I even begin?"

These doubts are normal, but they don't define you. Your voice matters, and your message is important. You've already done the hard work of writing and publishing your book, and now it's time to ensure it reaches the people who need it most.

I wrote this book because I believe in the power of books to change lives, not just for the people who read them and the communities they inspire but also for the authors who write them. Please keep me posted on your progress. You can always reach me at jgrace@publishyourpurpose.com. Let's work together to ensure your book isn't just written but is a tool that amplifies your voice, drives meaningful change, and leaves a legacy you're proud of.

INTRODUCTION

When I think about the process of promoting a book, it's clear to me that success isn't just about having a great idea. It's about creating habits and systems that ensure a story reaches the people who need it most.

When I wrote my first book, I quickly learned inspiration would take me only so far. The real transformation—the impact I hoped my book would have—came from persistence, preparation, and most importantly a strategy. Much of the anxiety new authors feel comes not from what they know they'll face but from the surprises they can't yet imagine. That's why this book lays out the full journey, not just the highlights.

If you've already read my last book, *Publish Your Purpose*, you may find parts of this one, especially chapters 1–4 and chapter 6, feel familiar. That's intentional. These chapters have been reframed, updated, and rewritten to focus specifically on marketing, visibility, and long-term impact. While the core ideas remain rooted in purpose-driven authorship, the guidance here is designed to take you further. If you come across content you've seen before, feel free to skim or skip ahead. This book is built to support both new and returning readers.

Not a One-Time Event

For many authors, publishing a book feels like crossing a finish line. Maybe that's you. You've poured your heart into writing, editing, and getting your story out into the world. But publishing is only the beginning. The real work, the work of amplifying your message and creating meaningful change, comes after the book is printed.

Writing a book has a start and a finish line, as does publishing one. But marketing a book? That's a race with a start line but no finish. Marketing is ongoing. It evolves as you grow, as your audience grows, and as your purpose grows. It's not a sprint; it's a rhythm.

That might feel overwhelming at first, but it's also a tremendous opportunity, and this book will help you make the most of it. Whether you've written a nonfiction book to share your thought leadership or a memoir to tell your story, and whether you're aiming to showcase your expertise, share personal lessons, or blend both, this book is for you. No matter your genre or your goals, the principles here are designed to help you use your book as a tool for impact. You've done the work, and now it's time to focus on what comes next: transforming your book into a platform for greater influence, deeper connection, and lasting change. This book gives you the strategy to do exactly that.

Laying the Foundation

Before we dive into strategy, it's essential to build a strong foundation rooted in confidence, clarity, and purpose.

1. You'll start by defining why your book matters, both to you and to the readers you're here to serve. This is your purpose and your vision, and together they form the compass that guides every marketing decision you'll make.

2. You'll then set meaningful and strategic goals that align with your vision so that you can track your progress, stay motivated, and know exactly what success looks like for you.

3. Equally important is your mindset. You'll shift the way you think about marketing, reframing it as an act of service, not self-promotion, so you can show up with confidence, clarity, and conviction. This mindset work will also help you move past imposter syndrome and into purposeful visibility.

4. With the right mindset in play, you'll then strengthen your support system. Having a network of peers, mentors, and accountability partners can make the difference between feeling isolated and feeling unstoppable.

5. You'll then explore how your book fits into a broader ecosystem of offers, services, and messages so that it becomes not just a product but a platform for influence and income. Whether you're growing an existing offering or using your book to launch something entirely new, you'll begin to map out how your book fits into your larger business model or brand.

6. As part of your book's ecosystem, you'll clarify exactly who your reader is and who's most likely to buy your book so that your marketing efforts speak directly to the people you're here to reach.

7. Finally, you'll learn how to lead with service instead of self-promoting, which will allow you to market with authenticity and build a more genuine connection with your audience.

With this foundation in place, you'll be equipped to move forward with confidence, clarity, and purpose, ready to build a marketing strategy that feels aligned with who you are and the change you want to create.

The ASPEN Method Framework

In part 2, we'll dive into the ASPEN Method framework: Assess, Strategize, Plan, Execute, and Nurture. Using this adaptable process, I'll guide you through developing a marketing strategy that aligns with your purpose and vision and helps you achieve your goals.

ASSESS   STRATEGIZE   PLAN   EXECUTE   NURTURE

What makes this approach unique is its flexibility. As we map out your marketing strategy, this book will introduce a "Pick Your Path" approach, but rather than including every possible tactic here, we've created a fresh and dynamic resource online. Not all strategies are relevant to every author, and trying to cover them all in one book would be overwhelming. So instead you can find a full library of tactical options that are aligned with each phase of the ASPEN Method and tailored to different book goals, audiences, and marketing styles

PICK YOUR PATH

on our website at promoteyourpurposebook.com/bonuses. This format allows you to customize your journey by choosing only the strategies that align with your particular purpose, audience, and goals, while this book remains focused on the foundational guidance you need to succeed.

Along the way, you might discover areas where your book's messaging or marketing strategy needs refinement. That's part of the process, and this book will guide you through realigning your goals when necessary to stay true to your purpose.

Putting It All Together

At the end of each chapter is a "Take Action" section, where I offer tools to track your progress and measure your success so you can keep your efforts intentional, effective, and aligned with your goals. These sections will become integral parts of your Strategic Book Marketing Plan, which you will develop as we go. Each chapter concludes with an inspiring call to action designed to help you take a focused, strategic step—one that aligns with your vision and moves you meaningfully closer to your purpose. Whether you compile your work in the space provided throughout this book, a separate notebook, or the online workbook, you'll leave this process with clear direction and actionable next steps.

TAKE ACTION

I often hear authors ask, "Why would anyone care about my book?" or "How can I promote my book without feeling pushy or salesy?" As you move forward, let me assure you: Your story has power. The work you've done to write your book, to share your ideas, expertise, and perspective, is already a gift to the world. Now your goal is to ensure that the right people discover it.

This isn't just about selling copies or gaining followers (although those are nice outcomes). It's about using your book as a tool to amplify your voice, establish your credibility, and create lasting impact.

Committing to the Journey

I know promoting your book can feel overwhelming. You might be wondering where to even start or whether you have the time or resources to do this. Here's what I want you to know: You do not have to have it all figured out today. The most important thing is to commit to the journey. We'll take it step-by-step, and I'll share tools, tips, and real-life examples to help you see what's possible. As you read, I hope you'll feel empowered to step into your role as a thought leader and change-maker.

If you're ready to take the next step in your journey—if you're ready to amplify your voice, grow your impact, and leave a legacy—then let's dive in and discover how to promote your purpose.

> You do not have to have it all figured out today. The most important thing is to commit to the journey.

PSA: The Em Dash Did Not Start with ChatGPT

Let's set the record straight: The em dash (—) has been around since the 1600s,[1] which is centuries before AI, the internet, or even indoor plumbing. It did not start with ChatGPT, and it certainly won't end there.

As for me? The em dash has been my favorite punctuation mark since I published my first book in 2013. I use it in everything—emails, social media posts, articles, and yes, even in texts! I use it because it's clear, flexible, and honestly kind of perfect.

So yes, you *will* see many of them in this book. That's not a glitch and it's not AI. That's just me writing the way I always have, consistently and unapologetically.

And for the record, the people who really love em dashes? We have the keyboard shortcut memorized.

---

1. T. Julian Brown, "punctuation," *Britannica*, last modified May 4, 2025, https://www.britannica.com/topic/punctuation.

PART 1
BUILDING YOUR FOUNDATION

Welcome to part 1. The following chapters lay the groundwork for your book promotion journey, starting with defining your purpose, vision, and impact. You'll uncover why you wrote your book and the change you aim to create, and you'll use those insights to guide your decisions and keep you motivated. You'll also explore the importance of accountability and support systems, clarify your goals, explore how your book fits into your broader ecosystem, and examine different business models that support sustainable growth.

We'll also address a critical (and often overlooked) topic: sales. Writing a great book isn't enough. You also need the confidence and tools to sell your services and offers with clarity and integrity, so you'll learn why sales skills are essential for purpose-driven authors and how to develop a selling approach that aligns with your values.

Whether you're expanding an existing business or launching something new, these chapters will help you align your marketing strategy with your long-term vision, equipping you with the tools and community needed to stay focused, consistent, and inspired.

CHAPTER 1
Clarify Your Purpose, Vision, and Impact

Welcome to the start of your book promotion journey. Writing and publishing your book required intention and focus, and promoting it demands the same dedication.

At Publish Your Purpose (PYP), purpose has always been at the core of everything we do, whether we're guiding authors through publishing or helping them amplify their messages through marketing. That's because purpose is the foundation of promotion. It's what drives your decisions, clarifies your direction, grounds you, and keeps you moving forward, especially when marketing feels overwhelming. The same way it grounded you during the writing process, your purpose will serve as the compass for your promotional efforts.

According to Dictionary.com, purpose as a noun is defined as "the reason for which something exists or is done, made, or used."[2] When you're promoting your book, keeping your purpose front and center helps align your actions with the change you hope to create, ensuring your marketing efforts stay grounded, intentional, and true to the message you're sharing. So I have a different definition for purpose: the intentional alignment of values, voice, and actions in service of a greater impact, both personal and collective.

---

2. Dictionary.com, "purpose," accessed June 26, 2025, https://www.dictionary.com/browse/purpose.

PROMOTE YOUR PURPOSE

Finding Your Purpose

What if you're not sure what your purpose is? What if it feels vague or surface-level?

That's completely normal.

Purpose is something that can take time and reflection to uncover. Take this time to center yourself in your *why*, the reason you've chosen to write, publish, and now promote your book. Your answers don't need to be solely outwardly focused. Think about your goals for yourself, too. Why does this book matter to you?

To make this exercise a little easier, here are a few inspiring examples from authors we've worked with:

- ▸ Jordan shared her experience as a family caregiver during a loved one's cancer journey. After his passing, she honored his story and now helps others navigate the emotional, logistical, and personal challenges of supporting someone through serious illness.

- ▸ Olivia is helping women in executive roles thrive on their own terms, using her book as a roadmap to empower a new generation of leaders to lead with confidence, authenticity, and lasting impact.

- ▸ Evan is using their lived experience of navigating life with a disability to advocate for systemic change. Their book shines a light on the barriers they've faced and provides tangible strategies for organizations and communities to become more accessible and inclusive.

- ▸ Thomas has spent more than 50 years supporting business owners. Now he's capturing the frameworks and lessons he's developed over decades and putting them into a book, creating a lasting resource to guide the next generation of entrepreneurs.

Another author I worked with shared a powerful realization about purpose. She had spent years building a career she was proud of, but one day she realized she'd been dedicating her energy toward advancing someone else's purpose, not her own. Now she's ready to channel her talents, passion, and experience into her own mission and message. Stories like hers remind us that it's never too late to realign your work with your true purpose. Whether you've always known what drives you or you're just beginning to reclaim your voice, your book is a way to plant your flag and say, "This is what I'm here for."

Your Purpose Doesn't Have to Be Grand (Yet)

Not everyone begins their book or business with a big vision to change the world. And that's okay. Your purpose doesn't have to be grand or world-changing to matter. It simply has to be meaningful to you. Sometimes your initial purpose is simple: get out of a toxic job, pay the bills, or reclaim your time. If that's where you are, you're in good company. Many thought leaders I've worked with began their journeys not with a clear business plan but with a feeling: *I can't do this the old way anymore.*

Purpose evolves over time. It deepens as your values become clearer and your confidence grows. It's okay to begin with survival. Or flexibility. Or freedom. Those starting points can still lead to tremendous impact, but only if you give yourself permission to begin. The key is to root your book and your goals in *honesty*, not in what looks good on paper. When your goals reflect what you truly want, not on what you *think* you should want, your marketing becomes more aligned, more effective, and more sustainable.

By exploring your purpose in depth, you'll not only gain clarity but also develop a sense of resilience. When marketing feels overwhelming or progress is slow, reconnecting with your why will remind you of the importance of your work.

What's Your Why?

This series of questions is designed to help you determine your why. Don't stop at the surface. Ask yourself each question two more times to dig deeper. This will help you uncover your purpose in a more meaningful way.

- ✓ **Why did you write this book?**

    But why?

    Okay, but why?

- ✓ **Why was it important to put your story into the form of a published book?**

    But why?

    Okay, but why?

- ✓ **Why does this book matter in *your* life?**

    But why?

    Okay, but why?

- ✓ **Why does this book matter in your *readers'* lives?**

    But why?

    Okay, but why?

- ✓ **Why are you committed to promoting this book?**

    But why?

    Okay, but why?

The answers you've come up with will act as your North Star, guiding your marketing decisions and keeping you aligned when challenges arise. If you need to revisit this exercise, do so. Do it as many times as needed to feel connected to your purpose.

Your Purpose in Action

Your core purpose serves as the foundation for everything you do, whether it's writing, publishing, or marketing your book. As my friend and story doula, Eduardo Placer, founder of Fearless Communicators says, "In both your speaking voice and your writing voice, there is a voice—and that voice is your voice." Whether we're writing our truths or speaking them from the stage, the most powerful thing we can do is show up authentically. Eduardo reminds us that specificity is what creates connection: "The more I speak to the specificity of my pain, the more you're able to universalize that as a reader, build empathy, and make your own connections."

My own journey with writing has reinforced the importance of having a clear purpose to guide both the creative and promotional processes. For example, when I wrote my fifth book, *Beyond the Rainbow*, my goal was to consolidate my decade of experience in LGBTQ+ marketing and consulting into a definitive resource. It was my way of ensuring the knowledge I'd gathered could continue to help others, even after I closed my consulting business. Once the book was out in the world, I knew I had shared everything I could, which allowed me to shift my energy fully into publishing the books of others.

Similarly, my previous book, *Publish Your Purpose*, was born out of my desire to make the publishing process more transparent and accessible. I wanted first-time authors to have a true step-by-step guide for writing and publishing their books whether they worked with my company or not. It was my way of leveling the playing field and empowering more people to confidently take the next step toward authorship.

My memoir, *House on Fire*, had a very different purpose. Unlike my nonfiction books, for which I had clear objectives for how they would serve my readers and my business, my memoir had only one goal: to help others feel seen and heard. I didn't write it with a marketing strategy in mind. Instead, I let the book itself dictate where it wanted to go. This approach led to deeply meaningful conversations, including one with a woman in Indiana who tearfully shared that—for the first time—she saw her own family reflected in a book. That moment reinforced the power of storytelling and the impact a book can have when it reaches the right audience.

Your purpose will look different from mine, and that's okay. What matters is that it feels authentic to you. Defining your why helps you push through challenges and will shape how you approach marketing your book. More than just selling copies, promotion is about ensuring your book reaches the right people and makes the impact you intended.

Your Vision

Now that we've explored the purpose behind promoting your book, let's dive into your vision.

I often ask authors, "If you could wave a magic wand and have your book in the hands of your ideal readers today, what is it doing for them? What is it doing for you?"

Similar to uncovering your purpose, you may not have a fully formed vision yet, and that's okay too. We're on this journey together, and throughout these next chapters we'll work through the process of defining what success looks like for you.

Your Life

When I ask you about your vision, I'm not just talking about your book's success. I mean your life as a whole. What impact do you hope promoting your book will have on your life? If you're not sure, start by asking yourself these questions:

- Do you imagine yourself traveling the world as a sought-after speaker?
- Do you want to create a steady stream of passive income so you can spend more time with your family?
- Are you hoping to build a strong personal brand that opens new doors for future opportunities?

If you struggle with envisioning your future, know that you're not alone. It took me years to allow myself to dream big instead of focusing on daily survival. If this resonates with you, talk with a trusted friend, mentor, or coach and brainstorm what your ideal future looks like (this also might be an opportunity to brainstorm with AI).

Your Business

Your book is a tool that can open doors, introduce you to new audiences, and create revenue streams beyond book sales. When forming your vision, think about your answers to these questions:

- What do you want book promotion to do for your business or career?
- Do you want your book to establish you as an authority in your industry?
- Are you hoping your book will lead to consulting opportunities, speaking engagements, or corporate partnerships?
- Are you using your book to build a coaching program, membership community, or online course?

Your Impact

Your book has the power to change lives, but only if it reaches the right people. Defining the impact you want to create will shape how you market your book and who you market it to. Ask yourself, "What do I want my readers to walk away with?" Here are two ideas to help get you thinking:

- If your book is about leadership, your marketing could focus on building a movement around ethical leadership.
- If your book is about mental health, your marketing might provide a safe space for open, honest conversations.

Remember: Marketing isn't just about selling books. It's about creating connections, building a community, and making a difference. Keep your vision front and center, and let it guide every decision you make.

The Work Is Your Evolution

Your book is more than just words on a page. It's your opportunity to create lasting impact. And as you clarify your purpose and vision, remember: You aren't just promoting your book, you're building a new version of yourself.

Your book doesn't live in a vacuum; it lives within your ecosystem. For some, that ecosystem includes speaking, while for others it's consulting, coaching, facilitating, training, or community-building. Your book makes you more visible, yes, but it also makes you more trustworthy. It shows people what you believe, how you think, and what it might feel like to work with you. It's not just something you sell; it's something you stand on.

When you promote your purpose, you're doing more than growing your business or selling your book. You're shaping the future by creating new possibilities for others to follow, learn from, and expand upon. Your book is not just a product; it's part of a larger ecosystem of change. Every time you share your story, and with every client you serve and every audience you inspire, you're leaving a legacy. You're building systems, ideas, and opportunities that ripple far beyond your immediate reach. The true heart of purpose-driven work is knowing your influence doesn't end with you but lives on in the people, communities, and movements you touch.

The true heart of purpose-driven work is knowing your influence doesn't end with you but lives on in the people, communities, and movements you touch.

PROMOTE YOUR PURPOSE

Purpose, vision, and impact are not abstract concepts. They're the foundations of every marketing decision you'll make. They'll ground your efforts, guide your strategies, and keep you moving forward, even when the path ahead feels uncertain.

Take immediate action by writing down your answers from the What's Your Why? section of this chapter, either here, in your own notebook, or in the online workbook. Next, write two or three sentences that capture your purpose, vision, and intended impact as an author. Keep it simple but true to you. This statement will serve as your compass for every decision you make throughout your marketing journey, so keep these visible, whether on your desk, a vision board, or a note on your phone, and revisit them weekly. Use them as a compass to evaluate your marketing efforts, continuing to ask yourself these questions:

What is my understanding of my why?

....

....

....

....

....

....

CLARIFY YOUR PURPOSE, VISION, AND IMPACT

How does this why align with my purpose?

....

....

....

....

How will my purpose move me closer to my vision?

....

....

....

....

Momentum builds with consistent action. Don't wait to feel "ready." Start today by setting one small, actionable goal, whether it's posting your first social media update, reaching out to a potential partner, or outlining a webinar. Every step you take reinforces your commitment to your purpose and your audience, and that commitment is what will drive your Strategic Book Marketing Plan.

> **PUT PURPOSE INTO PRACTICE**
>
> Reflect on your reason for writing the book you're promoting. Who do you want to reach, and what change do you want to spark? Write two to three sentences that capture your core purpose and vision. This can also serve as a starting point for your marketing messaging.

CHAPTER 2
Set Strategic Goals That Drive Real Change

Just as understanding your purpose, vision, and intended impact is critical, having clear goals for your book's promotion is essential. Without clear goals, it's easy to get lost in tactics that don't yield results or to feel overwhelmed by all the possible promotional avenues. Setting goals ensures your marketing strategy aligns with your expectations, and strong goals keep your marketing efforts intentional, ensuring that every step you take moves your book closer to the success you envision.

How you define success for your book will determine how you approach marketing it, and you can't measure what you don't track. So let's think about your goals for promoting your book. What do you hope to achieve?

- Land on a bestseller list?
- Be an award-winning author?
- Sell 10,000 copies?
- Reach one person whose life will be changed by your book?
- Get higher-paid speaking engagements?
- Bring in new business, consulting, or coaching clients?

If one of your goals includes raising your visibility, whether through speaking, coaching, consulting, training, or another form of thought leadership, this chapter will walk you through how your book supports that path. Your book can open doors to keynotes, workshops, podcast features, or paid partnerships, and even to launching new programs. From pricing your services to building your platform, these methods and ideas are designed to help you build a presence that drives both credibility and revenue. If something doesn't align with your immediate priorities, feel free to skim this chapter and revisit it when the timing fits.

Define Success on Your Terms

Your goals are personal to you. While it's helpful to hear advice from others, the most important thing is to define success in a way that makes sense for you, your book, and your purpose.

Think about what you hope to achieve and what marketing goals will help you get there. This is not about following generic success metrics or seeking validation from others but about defining what success looks like for your book's promotion. Whether your goal is to become a bestseller, generate business opportunities, or expand your reach, adding measurable outcomes will increase the likelihood of achieving it. And by making your goal more specific and aligned with your marketing strategy, you can create a targeted plan that maximizes your book's impact.

When setting your goals, do not chase vanity metrics. It's easy to get distracted by social media likes, follower counts, or viral content. While those numbers may feel validating in the moment, they don't always translate to real results. Visibility isn't the same as impact. Instead of fixating on metrics that look good on paper, focus on what actually moves your mission forward, such as pre-orders, speaking invitations, podcast interviews, email list growth, or strategic partnerships. Sustainable success is built on consistency, clarity, and connection, not quick hits. Let your metrics reflect what matters most to you.

Visibility isn't about shouting. It's about creating momentum through connection.

Make Your Goals Work for You, Not Against You

You might be familiar with SMART goals already, but let's view this through the lens of marketing your book. SMART is an acronym for specific, measurable, attainable, realistic, and timely. Let's run one of our sample goals through this test:

I want my book to appear on a bestseller list.

- **Is This Specific?**

    Yes and no. It's clear the goal is to get on a bestseller list, but it's not clear about which bestseller list.

- **Is This Measurable?**

    Yes and no. In a way it is because there are some loose metrics around what it takes to be on a bestseller list. But without knowing which list you're aiming for, you may not know exactly how many sales are needed or what else it might take to get there.

- **Is This Attainable?**

    Yes and no. If you're aiming to be on an Amazon bestselling list, the answer is yes. There's a clear process to follow to have your book be an Amazon bestseller. If you're aiming to be on *The New York Times* bestseller list, however, that's more like trying to catch lightning in a bottle. It's going to be hard, and attainability is going to depend on you, your platform, and your marketing and sales skills, among other things.

- **Is This Realistic?**

    Yes and no. If you're aiming to be on an Amazon bestselling list, the answer is yes, like before, since there's a clear formula to follow to make this happen. But you must spend the time and energy needed to learn that formula. And if you're aiming to be on *The New York Times* bestseller list, it will be trickier.

For a detailed breakdown of our Amazon Bestseller strategy, visit **promoteyourpurpose book.com/bonuses.**

If you have millions of followers with large platforms on social media as well as a big mailing list, then there's a chance this is a realistic goal for you. But if you don't have a large following or platform, that will likely put this goal into the unrealistic category.

- **Is This Timely?**
No. This isn't a time-bound goal because it doesn't specify when you'll do this. It could be assumed that you'll achieve this goal upon the launch of your book, but the goal doesn't state that specifically.

So let's reframe:

- **Old goal:** *I want my book to appear on a bestseller list.*

- **New goal:** I want my book to be #1 on the Amazon bestselling list in the Business & Leadership Category within one week of my book launching.

- **New goal:** I want my book to become a *New York Times* bestseller as soon as it launches, as I've grown a following of 500,000 people on my mailing list.

Now let's try this with a different kind of goal:

I want to expand my reach.

- **Is This Specific?**
Yes and no. It clearly states the desire to expand reach, but it doesn't define how, whether through social media, speaking engagements, media coverage, or another avenue.

- **Is This Measurable?**
No it's not. It lacks a specific number of people, platforms, or timeframe to gauge success.

- **Is This Attainable?**
Yes and no. Yes because expanding reach can happen in many ways, but no because defining the methods in which you plan to do so will make it more actionable.

- **Is This Realistic?**
  Yes, but without specifics it's difficult to determine what level of reach is achievable within a set timeframe.

- **Is This Timely?**
  No it's not. There are no parameters around this goal in terms of when this will happen.

So let's reframe:

- **Old goal:** *I want to expand my reach.*

- **New goal:** Within three months of my book launch, I want to grow my email list by 1,000 subscribers and secure five podcast interviews to introduce my book to new audiences.

See how a few small tweaks can turn a broad goal into something specific and actionable?

Align Your Book Description with Your Goals

As you clarify your goals, it's a good time to revisit your book description, the summary that appears on your back cover, your website, your book's listing on your publisher's website, and online retailer listings. Once your book is published, your book description is one of the first ways potential readers and clients learn what your book is about and who it's for.

In this book's companion workbook (or grab a notebook), you'll find space to drop in your current book description and reflect on whether it still aligns with your message, audience, and business goals, as well as with your vision for promotion. You don't need to rewrite it, but it's worth making sure it's still working for you, not just describing you. And if it's not, there's no time like the present to make a change.

Understand the "Why" Behind Your Goals

As with defining your purpose, it's essential to dig deeper into why you're setting specific marketing goals. This helps ensure your goals are rooted in purpose, not just external validation.

Take the goal *I want my book to be a bestseller* and ask yourself why, then again ask why after each of your responses. Here's an example to get you started:

- "Because I want people to recognize my book as successful." Why?
- "Because I want credibility in my field." Why?
- "Because I know my content is valuable, and I want my audience to trust my expertise." Why?
- "Because I feel like I need more visibility to grow my business." Why?
- "Because I want more clients and speaking opportunities."

After asking why multiple times, you might realize your true goal isn't about bestseller status but about increasing visibility and credibility. This could shift your marketing strategy to focus on guest podcast interviews, written thought leadership, or targeted business outreach rather than chasing a bestseller list.

Expand Your Influence

Once you've clarified your goals and the deeper reasons behind them, the next step is to explore how to translate them into concrete marketing goals that expand your influence.

While publishing a book elevates your credibility by positioning you as a thought leader in your field, a well-marketed book can attract speaking opportunities, media coverage, consulting clients, business partnerships, or personal connections. This makes your book a tool that can propel you, your career, or your business forward, but only if you actively promote it to open doors. The door you will walk through depends on your purpose and vision as well as the goals you've set, but there are some primary avenues.

PROMOTE YOUR PURPOSE

Your Book as a Springboard for Visibility

Whether your goal is to grow or launch a speaking career or start a coaching practice, consulting firm, training program, or visibility-based business, your book can serve as a powerful calling card. If speaking is part of your business model, or if you want it to be, your book is often the door-opener that gets you into the room. It helps you stand out in competitive speaker selection processes and gives event organizers confidence in your credibility. Think beyond book sales here. Could your book help you get on stage? If so, where? What keynote topics or breakout sessions could it support?

Regardless of what you're pitching yourself for, having a book positions you as a subject matter expert and trusted voice. You can leverage your book for that influence and visibility in ways other than speaking, and the most common I see are these:

> Remember: Not every speaking opportunity comes with a check, but that doesn't mean each isn't valuable. If a conference or organization doesn't have a speaker budget, make it a goal to see what else you can negotiate. Can they cover travel or accommodations? Will they buy books for the audience? Can you host a book signing, receive a vendor table, or be featured in their marketing materials?

- ▸ Use your book to pitch yourself for corporate trainings, consultations, client projects, or strategic partnerships.
- ▸ Secure guest appearances on podcasts where you can discuss your book's message and expertise, or spread the word via other media outlets.
- ▸ Collaborate with organizations or influencers who align with your book's purpose and are your strategic partners.
- ▸ Write articles, create social media posts, or produce videos that tie back to your book's themes.
- ▸ Apply to speak at TEDx or similar events where your book's message aligns with the event's focus on big ideas and community impact.

These moments are about more than exposure; they're about positioning. When leveraged well, even unpaid gigs can lead to bigger opportunities. The key is to show up professionally, add value, and ensure your presence plants seeds for the future. Your goal isn't just to "fill a slot" but to build a reputation.

Your Book as a Revenue Stream

If your book is meant to support your business or brand, financial goals should be part of your marketing strategy. While some authors focus solely on impact, others want their books to generate revenue, whether through direct sales, speaking engagements, or new business opportunities. Here are some SMART financial goals:

- I want to sell 5,000 copies in the first three months to generate $35,000 in revenue.
- I want my book to bring in new consulting clients and add at least $100,000 in business revenue within a year.
- I want my book to raise my speaking or consulting fee from $5,000 to $10,000 per engagement within a year by positioning me as a thought leader.
- I want my book to break even on my $20,000+ publishing and/or marketing investment within six months.

By setting clear financial goals, you can tailor your Strategic Book Marketing Plan to prioritize revenue-generating strategies, such as targeting corporate partnerships, leveraging email marketing, or using paid advertising.

I did this back in 2015 when I used strategic speaking and book placement to gain a meaningful return on investment (ROI). I was invited to speak on a panel at a high-level marketing leadership conference in Napa Valley, attended by 400 chief marketing officers—my exact target audience at the time. Ahead of the event, I asked the organizer if I could include a copy of my book in each attendee's conference bag. Printing and shipping 400 copies cost me about $2,000.

That one strategic investment paid off immediately.

Before the three-day event ended, two attendees hired me for consulting contracts totaling over $10,000. That not only covered the upfront cost but also led to two additional client referrals shortly after, which resulted in another $10,000. The ROI wasn't just financial. It built instant trust, visibility, and momentum for my business.

This example shows that a book isn't just a product. In the right rooms with the right goals and strategies, it becomes a tool for relationship-building and business growth that continues well beyond the first conversation.

Your Book as a Business Growth Tool

For many aspiring thought leaders, publishing a book is just one part of a bigger shift. You might be using your book to amplify an existing business, or maybe your goal is to use it as a springboard to launch something entirely new. No matter which path you're on, your book can serve as the credibility engine that powers the next phase of your work.

If your book is connected to your existing business, brand, or career, that should be a core part of your overall marketing strategy, not just a stand-alone project. Consider how your book fits into your larger ecosystem:

- Do you run a service-based business? Your book can serve as a lead generator for potential clients.
- Are you a consultant or speaker? Your book can boost credibility and justify higher fees.
- Do you have an online course or program? Your book can direct readers to your paid offerings.
- Do you produce content for a blog, podcast, or social media? Your book can reinforce your message and deepen engagement.

When your book is strategically aligned with your business, every promotional effort supports your long-term goals:

- It becomes the foundation for keynotes, workshops, or training sessions.
- It establishes your expertise and helps event organizers see you as a thought leader.

- It clarifies your point of view and methodology, making it easier for potential clients to understand how you can help.
- It shows the transformation you offer and builds trust with those considering a more personal, relational engagement.
- It introduces a broader audience to your work by creating low-barrier entry points to paid programs or recurring revenue opportunities.

Your Book as a New Business Launchpad

If your goal is to shift into something entirely new, such as a speaking career, coaching practice, consulting firm, or training program, you can use your book as a launchpad. Let's be honest. Starting a business is hard, especially when you're building something new after a long, successful career in another field. It can feel like trading stability for uncertainty, like being a beginner all over again, like having to "prove yourself" despite everything you've already accomplished.

That's normal.

When your identity has been tied to a past title, whether as an executive, educator, nonprofit leader, or corporate professional, shifting into entrepreneurship can feel both exciting and deeply vulnerable. You're not just promoting a book, you're (re)introducing yourself to the world.

The good news is that your book gives you a head start. A well-positioned book clarifies your message, but it also opens doors and builds your authority. It gives prospective clients or event organizers a tangible way to get to know you. Your job is to intentionally align your book's marketing strategy with the business model you want to build.

If you're not sure what your business model looks like yet, that's okay. As we continue building the foundation for your Strategic Book Marketing Plan, I'll help you map out how your book could connect to your revenue streams, client journeys, and long-term goals. But for now, just know this: Your book isn't just a stand-alone product. It's a business asset. When used intentionally, it becomes the centerpiece of your thought leadership and the key to building a business that reflects who you are and what you're here to do.

Methods for Setting Strategic Goals

Setting strategic goals isn't just about doing more. It's about doing what matters most, and in a way that aligns with your values, energy, and audience. The following approaches offer practical, purpose-driven ways to shape your book marketing efforts with clarity, sustainability, and intention.

Be Different on Purpose

In a crowded marketplace, clarity beats cleverness. One of the most strategic marketing moves you can make is to clearly articulate what sets you apart. Market differentiation isn't about being better than others. It's about being distinct. Your voice, your values, your experience, and your approach all shape your positioning. What do you offer that no one else does quite the same way?

When setting your goals, remember that your book is more than an extension of your brand; it's a declaration of what you stand for. When you lean into that specificity, you become easier to find, refer, and remember. This isn't about being everything for everyone. It's about becoming magnetic to the people who need you most.

If you're building or expanding a business alongside your book, make sure your message reflects the difference you're here to make. Whether you're a memoirist helping others heal, a consultant challenging outdated systems, or a coach guiding personal breakthroughs, your differentiation is a strategic asset. Use it.

Blend the Personal with the Practical

Along the same lines as being different, your readers want your story, not just your expertise. They want to know who you are, why this matters to you, and how you've walked through the fire yourself. The most compelling books weave personal narrative and practical strategy together, letting readers see the human behind the message.

Whether you're writing about leadership, healing, entrepreneurship, or advocacy, your lived experience is what makes your guidance resonate. A data point may inform, but a story moves. By sharing both, you create a book that not only teaches but transforms, making it one of the most strategic goals you can set.

Design Around Your Life, Not the Lives of Others

You didn't write your book just to burn out while promoting it. And you don't need to contort your strategies to match someone else's version of success. One of the most strategic things you can do when setting your goals for promotion is build your Strategic Book Marketing Plan around your *actual life*.

M. Shannon Hernandez, founder of Joyful Business Revolution™, joined me for a LinkedIn Live session during which she taught attendees that the best business models start by putting "all the life things in first." She uses a "Joyful Work Calendar" to help entrepreneurs map out their days based on values: time for rest, creativity, family, and health. That's the opposite of how most of us were taught to work, but it's the only way to build something sustainable. When I built PYP, I structured it to align with my son's school schedule, and that flexibility wasn't a luxury, it was essential. It let me grow a business that felt aligned with how I wanted to live.

So before you set your goal at batching 30 social posts, pitching 10 podcasts, or planning a major book tour, ask yourself these questions:

- What time do I want to work?
- What activities drain me vs. energize me?
- What are my top three lifestyle values right now?

Then, build your outreach *around* your answers. Because the goal isn't just visibility or sales, it's longevity. You're promoting a purpose that serves you and the people you want to reach, and that kind of alignment is what leads to lasting impact.

Lead with Generosity, Then Leverage with Intention

Promoting your book isn't just about being seen but also about how you show up. One of the most overlooked marketing strategies is leading with genuine generosity. That means offering value first—before asking for anything in return.

If you're setting a goal to attend a conference, research potential clients, or network with event organizers, think, *What can I offer that helps them, even if they never hire me?* This could be any of the following:

- Sharing a relevant article or podcast episode
- Sending a free copy of your book (signed, with a thoughtful note)
- Offering an introduction to someone in your network
- Creating a tailored PDF or short video showing how your content could serve their audience

When you lead with generosity, you build trust and goodwill, which often circles back as future business. People remember how you made them feel. And when the timing is right, they're more likely to say yes.

> Download the Canva template to create your own QR-powered book card by visiting **promoteyourpurposebook.com/bonuses.**

Generosity doesn't mean giving everything away. It means being intentional about the energy you bring to your marketing, offering real value up front, and positioning yourself as someone they *want* to work with. And visibility isn't about shouting. It's about creating momentum through connection. A favorite tactic of mine is to print business cards with my book's cover on one side and a QR code on the other that links to a downloadable chapter or bonus content. You can use these at conferences or networking events to build your email list while creating curiosity about your book.

Small, strategic efforts over time build real momentum.

PROMOTE YOUR PURPOSE

Maximize Your Visibility

Speaking of conferences, whether you're on stage or simply attending, every event is a chance to grow your platform. Too often, authors assume visibility only comes from keynote slots or breakout sessions. But your presence alone can open doors if you set strategic goals and know how to work the room.

Before you go, research the attendee list or conference app and identify a shortlist of people who align with your mission or could be ideal partners, clients, or champions. Reach out personally, saying things like, "I saw you'll be attending [event]. I'd love to connect while we're there. I'm [your one-liner] and just published a book on [topic]." Schedule coffee meetings in advance with people you want to connect with.

If you're attending a conference and *not* speaking, make a plan to still be seen. Sit up front. Be the first to ask a thoughtful question during the Q&A, and introduce yourself with a strong tagline. Bring copies of your book, or better yet, offer to mail it to key contacts afterward.

Don't disappear after the event. Follow up and send thank-you notes. Offer resources to those you meet and ask them who else they think you should meet.

Conferences aren't just moments, they're launchpads when you treat them like long-game opportunities. Just as marketing isn't a one-time event, your visibility strategy should be ongoing, not one-and-done. You don't need a stage to stand out. You need a plan and the confidence to own your space.

Build a Sustainable Routine

Getting your book—and your voice—out into the world takes persistence. But hustle doesn't have to mean burnout. Instead of chasing every opportunity, build a routine that aligns with your energy, capacity, and goals. Think of it as a rhythm, not a scramble.

Start by identifying the types of goals that move the needle for you. Is it gaining visibility through client referrals or guest podcast interviews? Creating educational webinars? Running a booth at a conference? Writing strategic social content? Then carve out time weekly or monthly to pitch

SET STRATEGIC GOALS THAT DRIVE REAL CHANGE

yourself intentionally, whether that's sending five outreach emails, applying for podcast guest spots, following up with leads, or developing new offers such as speaking engagements, consulting projects, or training programs. Keep a spreadsheet or customer relationship management system of places you've pitched or want to pitch, key deadlines, and relevant contacts. Track your wins, follow up with warm leads, and revisit your materials quarterly to keep them fresh.

> Download the pitch tracking spreadsheet to stay organized, follow up with leads, and build consistent momentum by visiting **promoteyourpurposebook.com/bonuses**.

The goal here isn't to do it all but to do the right things consistently. Small, strategic efforts over time build real momentum. This is how you go from being seen once to being remembered and even hired.

Setting clear, strategic marketing goals ensures your book's success is measurable and achievable. Whether your priority is impact, revenue, or long-term influence, defining your goals early will shape your promotional plan and give your marketing efforts direction.

Using this space, your own notebook, or the online workbook, use this exercise to clarify your goals and translate them into an actionable marketing roadmap.

1. List your top three goals for your book's promotion. These could relate to visibility, impact, financial return, speaking opportunities, or business development.

Goal #1 ....

....

....

....

....

Goal #2 ....

....

....

....

SET STRATEGIC GOALS THAT DRIVE REAL CHANGE

Goal #3 ....

....

....

....

....

2. For each goal, use the SMART framework to refine it.
   - **Specific:** What exactly do you want to achieve?
   - **Measurable:** How will you know you've achieved it?
   - **Attainable:** Is this realistic given your resources and platform?
   - **Relevant:** Does this align with your broader purpose or business?
   - **Timely:** What's your deadline for this goal?

Example:
   - General goal: I want to get media attention for my book.
   - SMART goal: I will secure coverage in three media outlets that reach my target audience within the first two months of launch by pitching story ideas weekly and following up with warm contacts.

SMART Goal #1 ....

S ....

M ....

A ....

R ....

T ....

PROMOTE YOUR PURPOSE

SMART Goal #2 ....

S ....

M ....

A ....

R ....

T ....

SMART Goal #3 ....

S ....

M ....

A ....

R ....

T ....

3. Pause and reflect. Which of your goals feel the most aligned with your current energy, resources, and purpose? Which might need to be postponed or adjusted for later?

SET STRATEGIC GOALS THAT DRIVE REAL CHANGE

Now that your goals are defined and you understand how your book, and potentially your business, supports them, it's time to work on your mindset about marketing so you can bring them to life.

> **PUT PURPOSE INTO PRACTICE**
>
> Clear goals lead to clear actions. Now that you've identified your top three SMART goals, it's time to move from planning to doing. From these goals, choose the one that feels most aligned with your current energy, resources, and purpose. Don't overthink it, just pick the one that feels most doable today. Then, take one small and specific action toward that goal. Maybe it's as simple as emailing a podcast host you admire to pitch yourself as a guest. Momentum builds when you act, not when you wait. Progress doesn't have to be perfect. It just has to be consistent.

CHAPTER 3
Build a Marketing Mindset That Fuels Growth

It's now time to bring your purpose and vision back to the forefront as you carry your goals and step into the next phase: building a marketing mindset. I know. Some of you are already cringing. But that's the mindset we need to change.

Promoting your book isn't just about sales. It's about amplifying your message, building meaningful connections, and expanding your influence. Many authors feel daunted, uncomfortable, or even inauthentic when thinking about marketing. The process can feel overwhelming, especially when doubt creeps in. What if no one engages? What if your message doesn't land the way you hoped? These are common fears that can paralyze even the most confident authors. That's why your mindset is one of the most crucial tools in your marketing strategy.

Marketing is just as important as writing your book because without it your book may never reach the people who need it most. Writing your book was an act of dedication and creativity, but ensuring it reaches the right people requires a strong mindset—one that embraces visibility, confidence, and resilience. Just as you envisioned the role your book would play in your life and the lives of your readers, you must now apply that same clarity and intention to your marketing efforts.

Let's start shifting your mindset so you can confidently share your book in a way that aligns with your purpose and values. That way, when the time comes to promote your book, you will do so with purpose, conviction, and the belief that your message deserves to be heard.

The Role of Marketing in Your Book's Success

Publishing a book is one thing, but successfully marketing it is another challenge entirely. Many authors assume that if they work with a publisher, whether traditional, hybrid, or a self-publishing service provider, they will receive significant marketing support. The reality is that marketing falls primarily on the author. Even with large publishing houses, authors are expected to drive most of the promotional efforts. Without an intentional marketing strategy, even the most well-written books can struggle to find their audience.

But marketing doesn't have to be overwhelming, expensive, or overly complicated. It simply requires a thoughtful approach, one that aligns with your strengths, business goals, and audience.

Marketing Is Storytelling

A common struggle I see is that authors view marketing as purely self-promotional. It feels ego-driven, like shouting, "Me! Me! Me!" But what if you reframed marketing as *an extension of storytelling* instead? Marketing is simply another way to share your ideas, insights, and the transformation your book offers readers. When you focus on how your book helps people rather than on just making a sale, you'll begin to feel more comfortable and authentic in the process.

Many purpose-driven authors feel a real tension between authenticity and visibility. They don't want to come across as pushy or overly sales-focused, and that's completely valid. But talking about your book is not about self-promotion; it's about serving others. It's about connecting your book with the readers who need it most. The sooner you reframe marketing as the *service* it is rather than as self-promotion, the sooner you'll shift into a mindset of abundance, one that puts your readers' needs first.

When I talk with authors about this, one theme always emerges: They're far more comfortable promoting a purpose than pushing a product. We once worked with a group of authors so hesitant about marketing that we had to rebrand our strategy sessions as "Lighting Fire" because even the word *marketing* felt misaligned to them. That's how deeply ingrained this fear can be. A simple mindset shift from "pitching" to "inviting" changes everything. It aligns your values with your actions and helps you show up with more ease, confidence, and sincerity. Another reframe that helps is to think of marketing as an *invitation* rather than as self-promotion. You're not demanding attention, you're opening a door.

There's no right or wrong way to market a book, only what's aligned or not aligned for *you*. If a strategy feels forced or inauthentic, there's almost always another route that will still move the needle. Throughout this book, you'll explore a variety of marketing strategies and tactics designed to align with how you want to show up, and you'll have the opportunity to choose the approach that feels authentic to you. Regardless of the path you're taking, finding that alignment will transform your entire experience of book promotion.

Michael Losier, author of the bestselling book *Law of Attraction* and host of an Oprah Winfrey Network radio show by the same name, has sold millions of copies of his book and built a global platform around his message. Yet even he sees the importance of shifting the spotlight away from himself and onto his work. As he told me during our conversation, "Some people feel like impostors. They're worried, *Who am I to be talking about this?* But when you make the book the hero, you're not coming from such a vulnerable place. You're pointing to the message, not yourself." This reframe can be a turning point. You're not promoting yourself, you're promoting the solution, the insight, the story, or the strategy that lives inside your book. That mindset shift helps reduce fear, unlock confidence, and build a genuine connection with your audience.

So instead of worrying about *how* to market your book, focus on *why* you wrote it in the first place. Let that purpose guide your conversations, your content, and your outreach.

A Clear Plan of Action Reduces Overwhelm

Bringing a book into the world is an exciting milestone, but it can also feel like an uphill battle, especially when you realize that writing the book was just the beginning. Many authors struggle with how to market, sell, and position their book in a way that aligns with their broader goals. It's easy to feel scattered, unsure of what to prioritize, and overwhelmed by the sheer number of decisions that need to be made.

I recently had a conversation with an author who was experiencing exactly this. She had poured years into writing her book and building an entire ecosystem of resources around it, including a workbook, an e-learning course, and a keynote presentation, but she found herself stuck when it came to actually getting it into the hands of the right people. She wasn't lacking ideas or effort. What she lacked was a clear, repeatable plan. She knew where she wanted her book to go: bulk sales to large healthcare organizations, speaking engagements that would lead to book purchases, and long-term partnerships with mission-aligned companies. But despite attending the right conferences and networking in the right circles, she wasn't sure how to move from building relationships to closing sales. She also felt exhausted trying to juggle marketing, sales, content creation, and business development all at once.

This is a common experience among authors. Many are deeply passionate about their work but struggle with the logistical side of book promotion. They assume that if they just show up and talk about their book, the sales will follow. But without a structured system in place, even the most engaged audience can walk away without taking action.

What this author needed, and what most authors need, is a framework to simplify, systematize, and sustain the work of book promotion—a way to move from scattered efforts to a focused, step-by-step approach that feels manageable rather than overwhelming. She needed a clear way to translate her book's message into a structured sales process without feeling like she was constantly reinventing the wheel.

That's exactly why I created the ASPEN Method. It's a framework designed to help authors streamline their marketing and sales efforts, focus on what actually moves the needle, and create a long-term impact with their book. Instead of trying to do everything at once, the ASPEN Method framework breaks book promotion into manageable, strategic phases. It allows authors to prioritize their efforts, build a support system, and execute a plan that aligns with their unique goals. The goal isn't to do more, it's to do what matters most, consistently and effectively.

You're not promoting yourself, you're promoting the solution, the insight, the story, or the strategy that lives inside your book.

With the right strategy in place, you can transform your book from something you hope will gain traction into a powerful tool that actively supports your business, career, and mission. I'll walk you through the ASPEN Method framework in detail in part 2, but we must start with mindset, specifically the area that holds most authors back: imposter syndrome.

Overcoming Imposter Syndrome in Book Marketing

If you've ever felt hesitant about putting yourself out there, worried about what others will think, or convinced that no one will care about your book, welcome to imposter syndrome. It's that nagging voice in your head that whispers, "Who am I to market this book? What if people don't take me seriously? What if no one buys it?"

Psychology Today defines it this way: "People who struggle with imposter syndrome believe that they are undeserving of their achievements and the high esteem in which they are, in fact, generally held. They feel that they aren't as competent or intelligent as others might think—and that soon enough, people will discover the truth about them. Those with imposter syndrome . . . are often well accomplished; they may hold high office or have numerous academic degrees."[3] Based on my own personal experience with imposter syndrome, as well as having coached hundreds of people, many of whom also have it, this definition could not be any more accurate. It's a common struggle for high achievers, especially those stepping into new territory—like marketing their own book.

The truth is that imposter syndrome tends to show up whenever we take a bold step outside our comfort zones. Writing your book may have felt like a personal challenge, but promoting it requires a different kind of courage—the type that asks you to be seen, to take up space, and to advocate for the message you worked so hard to share.

---

3. "Imposter Syndrome," Psychology Today, accessed June 28, 2025, https://www.psychologytoday.com/us/basics/imposter-syndrome.

I've been where you are. The book you're reading now is the eighth one I've written, and despite more than a decade as an author, I've lost count of how many times I've questioned whether my work was good enough. Even as I write these words, that little voice in my head asks, "Will people find value in this?" But here's what I've learned: We're all imposters until we aren't, and the only way to quiet imposter syndrome is to take action anyway.

The fear of marketing your book won't disappear overnight, but it doesn't have to hold you back. The key is to recognize that your book has value, and not because you're the absolute, foremost expert in your field but because your unique perspective and experiences bring something important to the conversation. Your book doesn't have to be *the* book on the subject; it just has to be *your* book written in *your* voice for the people who need to hear it. Your unique angle is more than enough. Your experience is more than enough. You are enough. Reread this again if you're still struggling: You. Are. Enough.

When self-doubt creeps in, try these three mindset shifts to move forward with confidence:

1. **Reframe Marketing as Service, Not Self-Promotion**
   Marketing isn't about bragging. It's about making sure your book reaches the people who need it. Instead of asking, "What if no one buys it?" ask yourself, "What if the right person never finds it?"

2. **Focus on the Impact, Not the Outcome**
   Instead of stressing over sales numbers or social media engagement, ground yourself in the real reason you wrote your book: to help, inform, or inspire. When you lead with impact, marketing feels more meaningful.

3. **Take Small, Intentional Steps**
   Imposter syndrome thrives on inaction. The more you hesitate, the stronger it gets. Combat it by taking one small step today, such as sharing an excerpt, pitching yourself to a podcast, or posting about your book in a way that aligns with your values.

You don't have to be the world's leading expert to market your book successfully. You simply need to believe in its value and have the courage to share it.

When Your Work Keeps Evolving

One of the most common struggles I see with coaches, creatives, and entrepreneurs is the fear of confusing their audiences. Maybe you've been a grief guide, then an intuitive healer, then a health coach, and each identity aligned with where you were at the time. But now, looking back, it's hard to explain the full arc, and it's even harder for your audience to know what you actually do. If your career has followed a winding path, you're not alone. Many purpose-driven leaders I work with have worn a dozen hats over the years, including consultant, speaker, strategist, coach, healer, and facilitator.

In one of PYP's author training videos, Erin Weed, speaker, author, and founder of The Dig, says, "We all go through these shifts in our lives. And most people resist them because they think to themselves, *I don't know how to talk about this new version of myself.*" I agree, and this is where your book becomes essential. It's not just a calling card, it's your throughline. It's the one consistent narrative that connects your past to your present and to where you're going next. But more than that, your book has the power to tell the larger story behind all your pivots, the deeper why that has always driven your work, even as the expressions of that work have changed.

I often say to authors who are worried about wearing many hats, "Your book helps connect the dots between everything you do, making what might seem disjointed look like a clear, purposeful path." Because when your book is rooted in a bigger message—when it's a throughline that transcends job titles or service offerings—it becomes a map that others can follow. It allows people to see your evolution not as inconsistency but as integration. Without that kind of grounded narrative, your audience may see only the surface-level shifts. But with it, they understand the arc. They see the growth. They trust your journey, and they trust you.

> Authority comes from consistency, not from having everything figured out.

Your book gives context, clarity, and cohesion, and that is the heart of thought leadership. So when you're setting your goals, keep in mind that though the details may shift and your LinkedIn title may change, the core of your message often remains the same.

Here are some tips for navigating the shift:

- Reframe your story. You're not "starting from scratch," you're "evolving." Bring your past expertise into your new narrative.

- Use your book as a bridge. Let your book introduce your new message, methodology, or mission to the world.

- Lean on your community. Find others who've reinvented themselves and share openly about the transition.

- Don't wait for it to feel perfect. Show up with what you have now. Authority comes from consistency, not from having everything figured out.

If you've ever worried that your shifting identity is confusing your audience, your book can be the throughline that grounds it all. And when your audience can see the thread connecting everything you do, they're more likely to trust you, refer you, and invest in your work. That's why a book is so powerful: It creates consistency even when your career doesn't look linear. It's not just a business card or a product; it's a cohesive statement of values, expertise, and intention that allows your audience to track your evolution and still understand what you stand for.

Shift Your Mindset, Raise Your Rates

Though promoting your book is about far more than sales, it's important to at least think about ROI, and not just in dollars but in time, energy, and outcomes. Many authors pour money into book promotion without having clarity on what they're hoping to get back. Before you invest in ads, publicists, or speaking events, ask yourself these questions:

- What specific result do I want from this investment?
- How will I measure success?
- Will this activity bring me closer to my goals?

For example, if your goal is to generate $25,000 in consulting revenue from your book, then sponsoring a $5,000 conference booth might be worth it, especially if it puts you in front of the right decision-makers. But if your goal is visibility within a specific niche, a guest podcast appearance might bring more qualified leads for far less.

Being ROI-aware doesn't mean doing only what's profitable. It means being intentional about where you spend your resources so that you don't burn out or feel defeated. Strategic marketing is about balancing effort with outcomes that matter to you, whether that's revenue, reach, or long-term impact.

The biggest difference between experts who charge $1,000 and those who command $15,000 or more often isn't experience; it's mindset. Many purpose-driven speakers undercharge because they don't see themselves the way clients do: as experts offering immense value. If you're new to speaking, it's easy to default to "I'll take whatever they offer." But here's the truth: *You* set the bar. If you say your keynote rate is $5,000, people will assume that's your level. If you say $500, they'll believe that too.

It's okay to stretch into this. Your rate should make you feel a little nervous, like you're stepping into a bigger version of yourself. That's often where the growth begins. And if you're not ready to charge full price, you can still start high and negotiate strategically. For example, "My typical speaking fee is $5,000, but for this audience I'd be happy to discuss other value-based options." You can also make your request easier by removing yourself from the negotiation, such as using a booking assistant or even an AI tool with prewritten scripts to send your fee structure. This creates space for confidence to grow while still holding your value, and it positions you as someone who takes their work seriously.

Organizers aren't just hiring a speaker. They're protecting their own credibility. Your professionalism, preparedness, and message clarity make you the safe bet they can trust with their audience. You've invested in your expertise, and your book proves it. Don't discount what it's worth.

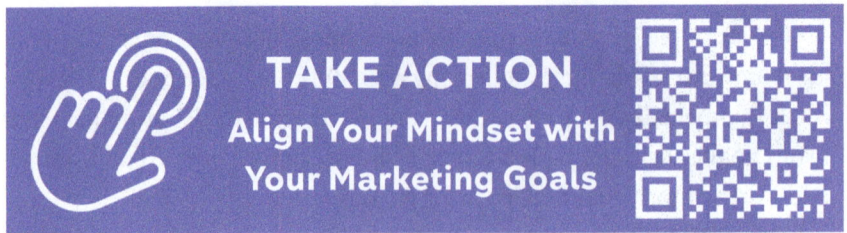

At the end of the day, your mindset can be a life raft or lighthouse that guides you through the challenges of book promotion. The key is to stay committed to your goal of getting your book into the hands of the right readers while maintaining balance and intention. Here are some ways to take action right now.

Craft a Tagline That Makes People Lean In

When you have just a few seconds to make an impression, whether you're introducing yourself at a conference or connecting online, a sharp, memorable tagline helps you stand out. Don't think of it as a sales pitch but as a positioning statement that invites curiosity and instantly conveys your value.

The most powerful taglines do three things:

1. Say what you do.
2. Hint at who you help.
3. Leave the listener wanting more.

Consider these real-world examples:

1. "I help organizations move beyond performance and profit toward an environment where everyone can breathe, lead, and thrive."
2. "I guide leaders through burnout toward purpose-driven action."
3. "I turn hidden stories into keynote messages that spark change."

Short, evocative, and clear, these taglines don't sell; instead, they invite the listener to ask questions or see themselves in your mission. They open a door to deeper conversations, just like your book does.

BUILD A MARKETING MINDSET THAT FUELS GROWTH

If you're struggling to write your own, start by brainstorming around these prompts:

- What's the core message of your book?
- Who do you want to reach or help?
- What change or transformation do you make possible?

Using this space, your own notebook, or the online workbook, take some time to craft your initial tagline.

My Initial Tagline: ....

....

....

....

....

....

Now, try boiling it down to a single sentence, aiming for no more than 10–12 words. Test it out in your introductions and see how people respond. When they lean in and say, "Tell me more," you'll know it's working.

My Refined Tagline: ....

....

....

....

....

....

Reaffirm Your Purpose

Marketing without purpose feels like pressure. But when you're grounded in why you wrote your book and who it's meant to serve, everything becomes more focused, and more fulfilling.

Write a short paragraph revisiting your core purpose:

- Why did you write this book?
- What change are you hoping to create?
- Who are you trying to reach?

My Core Purpose: ....

....

....

....

....

....

....

Keep this visible as a daily reminder when marketing feels overwhelming.

Shift Your Perspective on Marketing

Many authors carry limiting beliefs about visibility, especially when their work has evolved over time. They worry about seeming inconsistent, self-promotional, or unclear in their messaging. These doubts can quietly undermine even the strongest strategies, unless you address them head-on.

Let's change the story you're telling yourself. Here are a few common mindset traps and one empowering way to reframe each one. Use the space provided, a notebook, or the online workbook to write your own version based on your experience.

BUILD A MARKETING MINDSET THAT FUELS GROWTH

LIMITING BELIEF	EMPOWERED REFRAME	YOUR REFRAME
"I don't want to seem pushy."	"I'm making it easier for the right readers to find my work."	
"I'm not an expert; I'm still figuring it out."	"I have real-world experience and perspective people can learn from."	
"My message has changed too much."	"I've grown. My book brings it all together."	
"I hate promoting myself."	"I'm sharing a message that can help people."	
"Who am I to talk about this?"	"My lived experience is valuable. My story has power."	

Marketing your book is a marathon, not a sprint. Keep your mindset strong, celebrate your progress, and trust that your message deserves to be heard.

PUT PURPOSE INTO PRACTICE

Put your mindset into motion. Start by choosing one small action that aligns with your purpose, such as sharing a story, talking about your book, or practicing your tagline. Remember: Promotion is service, not self-promotion. Each step builds confidence. When doubt creeps in, return to your purpose. Let it guide how you show up and remind you why your message matters.

CHAPTER 4
Stay Motivated with Support, Structure, and Accountability

Marketing your book can feel just as lonely as writing it, if not more so. Many authors assume that once their book is published, the hardest part is over. But getting your book into the hands of readers requires just as much dedication and comes with its own set of emotional challenges.

Unlike writing, which is often a solo effort, marketing requires visibility, consistency, and engagement with others. It means putting yourself out there, showing up online, reaching out to potential collaborators, and asking people to buy, read, and talk about your book.

For some, this process is exciting because it's an opportunity to connect with their audiences in new ways. For others, it's terrifying. The fear of rejection, imposter syndrome, or feeling like they're "selling" can cause many authors to avoid marketing altogether. This is why accountability in book marketing is just as crucial as it was when you were writing. Having the right support system will keep you consistent, help you move past self-doubt, and ensure your book doesn't fade into the background after launch.

Let's explore how to build a marketing support system that can keep you on track, motivated, and strategic as you promote your book.

Your Marketing Support System

Having the right support system can make or break your book marketing success. Surrounding yourself with people who believe in you and will push you when you need it can be the difference between a book that gains momentum and one that disappears into the void.

> Your strategy isn't about showing up constantly. It's about showing up intentionally.

STAY MOTIVATED WITH SUPPORT, STRUCTURE, AND ACCOUNTABILITY

In my personal experience of having marketed my own books and coached hundreds of authors, I've found three types of people are essential to this process:

1. The Strategist, who helps you create and stick to your marketing plan
2. The Therapist, who helps you navigate self-doubt, fear, and rejection
3. The Cheerleader, who keeps you motivated and celebrates your progress

One person can fill multiple roles, or different people can support you in different ways. You won't need all three at every moment, but at some point in your marketing journey you will need each one. Let's go into more detail on each.

The Strategist: Your Marketing Guide

Your Strategist is the person who helps you see the big picture when it comes to marketing your book. This might be a marketing coach, book publicist, or business mentor, but it can also be an author friend who has successfully promoted their book. Their role is to help you answer questions like these:

- How do I reach my ideal readers?
- What's the best way to leverage my book to grow my business or brand?
- What are my key marketing milestones before and after launch?

Your Strategist will work with you to develop a concrete marketing plan based on your strengths and available resources. They'll help you identify several components:

- Which platforms or marketing channels will work best for you? (e.g., social media, speaking engagements, media interviews)
- How to pace your promotional efforts so that you don't burn out

- How to measure success beyond just book sales (e.g., growing your email list, increasing brand awareness, securing more speaking opportunities)

The Therapist: Your Emotional Foundation

Marketing a book brings up a lot of emotions, including self-doubt and fear. You'll need someone in your corner who can help you navigate these challenges. This doesn't have to be an actual therapist (though that can be helpful). It could be someone already in your circle:

- A business coach who helps you work through mindset blocks
- A trusted friend who listens when you're feeling discouraged
- A fellow author who understands the ups and downs of book promotion

When you start questioning yourself—Who am I to promote this book? What if no one buys it? Am I being too pushy?—your Therapist helps remind you why you wrote this book in the first place.

Even experienced professionals feel imposter syndrome. When the stakes feel high, it's normal to fantasize about being less visible, like getting a job stocking shelves. The nerves don't mean you're not cut out for this; they mean you care deeply about doing it well. They also help you deal with rejection. Not every pitch will be accepted, and not every reader will love your book. Marketing is about consistent effort, not immediate results, and having a support system will help you push through moments of self-doubt.

The Cheerleader: Your Motivational Boost

Your Cheerleader is the person who keeps you going when marketing feels exhausting. They might be one or more of the following:

- A friend or family member who reminds you how amazing your book is
- A writing group or marketing mastermind that holds you accountable
- A social media community that celebrates your small wins with you

Again, marketing is a marathon, not a sprint. When it feels like no one is paying attention, your Cheerleader will remind you that every post, every interview, and every conversation is building momentum.

Structure Your Success

Marketing can be unpredictable, and life will inevitably get in the way. That's why pre-planned responses to common roadblocks can help you stay on track. During an internal training session at PYP, visibility strategist N. Chloé Nwangwu wisely said, "What if your visibility isn't constant because you aren't meant to be constant? You're a human being, not a brand campaign. What should be consistent are the ideas you're sharing, not necessarily the social media posting."

At PYP, we've found a simple way to prepare you for how to handle life when it comes rolling at you at an inconvenient time: The "IF this, THEN that" statement. This statement is common in computer programming and can be a game changer for supporting your book because it helps you create strategies and keep your momentum. The good news is that it's very simple to create. Here are three examples:

1. IF I feel overwhelmed by social media marketing,
   THEN I will focus on one platform and outsource graphics.

2. IF I get discouraged by slow book sales,
   THEN I will focus on building my email list and engaging with my audience.

3. IF I struggle with imposter syndrome,
   THEN I will remind myself of one person who told me my book made an impact.

Do you see how having these pre-planned, structured statements can be simple yet powerful? It gives you space to predict what will distract you and to have a plan in place for what to do when that happens. This can be a game changer for getting you back on track when you inevitably fall off and into life's everyday pressures.

Remember: Your strategy isn't about showing up constantly. It's about showing up intentionally.

Accountability Partners and Marketing Check-Ins

While preparing for obstacles is key, having external accountability will push you even further. That's where accountability partners come in. Marketing is a long game, and consistent action beats perfection every time. Finding an accountability partner or marketing group can make all the difference.

> Looking for support and accountability? Join PYP's marketing groups and connect with authors promoting their books with purpose—**promoteyourpurposebook.com/bonuses.**

Here are some ideas for how to find a marketing accountability partner:

- Connect with fellow authors in online groups, LinkedIn, or writing communities.
- Partner with someone launching a book around the same time as you.
- Join a marketing mastermind or author support group.

And here's how to stay accountable:

- Set up weekly check-ins to track progress.
- Share marketing wins (big or small) with your partner.
- Encourage and challenge each other to step outside your comfort zones.

Marketing is a marathon, not a sprint.

PROMOTE YOUR PURPOSE

Your book was never meant to sit quietly in the background; it's meant to reach, impact, and inspire people. And marketing isn't about instant success; it's about showing up again and again until your book lands in the hands of those who need it most. Here's how to take action and put these ideas into motion right now (the following exercises are also available as a downloadable worksheet on the website; promoteyourpurposebook.com/bonuses):

My Support Team

Now that you know the three people you need in your support network, take a few minutes to fill in who will play these roles in your life as you promote your book.

STRATEGIST	THERAPIST	CHEERLEADER
1.	1.	1.
2.	2.	2.
3.	3.	3.
4.	4.	4.
5.	5.	5.

My Structured Backup Plans

Use the space provided or download the worksheet to work through some of your own personal examples of roadblocks and your pre-planned responses to them.

FILL IN THE BLANKS
IF: THEN:
IF: THEN:
IF: THEN:

PROMOTE YOUR PURPOSE

My Accountability

Identify one person you can regularly check in with about your book marketing progress. Find a marketing accountability partner and schedule your first check-in. Consistent action starts with consistent support. Use these steps to turn your marketing intentions into steady momentum.

Step 1: Write down the name of your accountability partner.

....

Step 2: Determine your check-in frequency.
- ☐ Weekly
- ☐ Biweekly
- ☐ Monthly

Step 3: Determine your preferred day.
- ☐ Monday
- ☐ Tuesday
- ☐ Wednesday
- ☐ Thursday
- ☐ Friday
- ☐ Saturday
- ☐ Sunday

Step 4: Determine your format.
- ☐ Text
- ☐ Email
- ☐ Video Call
- ☐ In-person

STAY MOTIVATED WITH SUPPORT, STRUCTURE, AND ACCOUNTABILITY

Your book deserves to be read. Your message matters. Stay accountable, keep going, and trust that your marketing efforts will lead to lasting impact. Your audience is waiting.

> **PUT PURPOSE INTO PRACTICE** Take an honest inventory of your current mindset around marketing. What limiting beliefs or fears are holding you back? Write down one belief you want to shift and one small action you'll take to move forward with more confidence, then reach out to your accountability partner today and ask them to walk this journey with you.

BOOK
Reviews & Testimonials
Courses or Companion Workbooks
Pre-Orders & Launch Events
Awards & Recognition
Academic Marketing

THOUGHT LEADERSHIP
Content Marketing
Social Media
Newsletters
Podcasts
PR & Media Outreach

YOUR AUTHOR ECOSYSTEM
Every anchor strengthens your purpose, impact, and visibility.

BUSINESS
Cause Marketing
Products & Services
Coaching / Consulting
Partnerships & Collaborations
Revenue Systems

SPEAKING
Signature Talks
Conferences & Events
Client Engagements
Book Clubs & Communities

CHAPTER 5: Turn Your Book Into an Ecosystem

A book is not an isolated product; rather, it's part of an ecosystem. That ecosystem extends far beyond the pages of your book. It's a dynamic, interconnected network with a broad framework that integrates personal branding, business objectives, thought leadership, and public engagement. At the heart of this ecosystem is you, the author, whose authenticity and personal brand shape every aspect of how the book was written and will be marketed and promoted.

The most effective book marketing strategies stem from your ability to remain true to your voice, ensuring that all forms of communication—written, spoken, digital, and in person—align with your unique personality and message. Just as your voice drives your book, your marketing strategy determines how that book will support your larger goals.

Your Ecosystem in Motion

As an author, surrounding you are four primary anchors that drive your book's success:

1. **The Book Itself**

    The book is the cornerstone of this ecosystem, but it's not the only valuable component. The content within the book can be strategically repurposed and expanded upon in various ways to reach different audiences and enhance your credibility and visibility.

2. **Thought Leadership**

    More than just a collection of ideas, a book is a platform for thought leadership. Each book contributes to a larger conversation, and whether through media appearances, blog writing, podcasting, or social media discussions, it positions you as a leading voice in your field.

3. **Business**
   For many authors, a book is more than just a passion project; it's a strategic tool to grow a business, enhance a personal brand, or create new career opportunities. A well-positioned book builds credibility, attracts clients, and opens doors to new partnerships.

4. **Speaking**
   Live events, workshops, and presentations create opportunities to extend the reach of your book's message. When you speak about the themes in your book, you reinforce your credibility and invite new audiences into your ecosystem.

Each of these anchors is supported by a range of marketing and promotional strategies that bring readers into your world and convert visibility into opportunity. These may include coaching or consulting services, courses, partnerships, media appearances, newsletters, or aligned social impact initiatives.

What's most important is that these strategies matter only when they align with your business model or personal vision. For example, if you're aiming for bulk book sales tied to speaking engagements, your marketing approach might be focused on securing speaking opportunities where book sales are part of the contract. If you're looking to drive new leads for a high-end service, your outreach strategy might be more personal, often involving third-party endorsements, strategic introductions, or customized proposals. And if your goal is to spark healing, raise awareness, or build community around a shared experience, your focus might be on fostering meaningful conversations, deepening trust, or reaching aligned partners who can help carry your message further.

Start with Your Business Model

If you've set your strategic goals to include leveraging your book for growing your business, you need to understand your business model first. This isn't just a question of whether you have one but of how clearly defined it is and whether your book fits seamlessly into it. Are you selling keynote talks or high-ticket consulting? Are you trying to fill group programs? Are you building a high-volume business that needs to reach a wide audience quickly, or are you working within a low-volume, high-trust model in which one new client every few months is enough?

Understanding this matters. A business that relies on volume (think public speaking, digital courses, or platform-driven marketing), requires consistent visibility and broad audience engagement. In contrast, a low-volume, high-trust business (think executive coaching, training, or large-scale consulting) benefits from deep relationships, fewer leads, and more personalized outreach.

When your business model is clear, the role your book plays in that model becomes clear too. In high-volume models, your book might be a lead magnet, a social proof tool, or the centerpiece of a funnel that converts readers into subscribers, then into buyers. In lower-volume models, your book might act more like a high-end calling card, something you physically hand to a potential client or collaborator to initiate deeper conversations and establish trust. In either case, your book will do the heavy lifting of positioning you as an expert and paving the way for what happens next in your business.

If you're unsure where you fall, start by asking yourself a few key questions:

- Do I need to attract large audiences to hit my goals, or can a few new, high-quality clients make a big difference for me?
- Am I focused more on broad reach and visibility or building deeper relationships with a smaller audience?

Your answers will help clarify how to position your book and help you determine which marketing strategies are most aligned with your goals moving forward.

A book is not an isolated product; rather, it's part of an ecosystem.

From Corporate Leader to Solo Business Owner: A Common Pivot

Imagine this: You've built a 20-year career in a corporate or nonprofit leadership role. You're well respected, and you've led teams, driven results, and built a reputation as the go-to expert in your field. But now you're ready for something different, something more aligned with your purpose.

So you write a book.

You pour your experience and expertise into it, hoping it will open new doors. And it does, but not in the linear way you expected. Suddenly you're no longer only "Director of Strategy" or "SVP of Operations" but are a published author, and people want more from you. A workshop. A keynote. A consultation. Maybe even a retreat or group coaching program.

And then it hits you: You've just started a new business.

But starting a business, especially after years of career success, can feel a bit like starting over. That's why I've included this topic: to help you get clear on how your book fits into your ecosystem, whether you're enhancing what you already have or building something brand new.

If you're in the process of launching a business, or even just entertaining the idea, creating a simple business plan can provide much-needed clarity. It doesn't have to be complex or formal. At its core, your business plan should articulate what you're offering, who it's for, how you'll deliver it, and how you'll generate revenue. This isn't about writing a 40-page document. Think of it as a strategic map that keeps you grounded as you move from idea to implementation. Include key elements such as your services, pricing strategy, revenue goals, target audience, and marketing channels, and consider how your book aligns with each one. The more intentional you are here, the easier it becomes to make aligned decisions and recognize opportunities as they arise.

What No One Tells You About Starting Over

Publishing a book is often a turning point, especially for authors transitioning into something new. Maybe you've left a long, successful career and are stepping into entrepreneurship for the first time. Maybe you're launching a coaching or consulting practice. Or maybe you're testing the waters of thought leadership through speaking. No matter the path, the transition is real, and so is the identity shift that comes with it.

Going from being an established expert in one field to a beginner in a new business can be both exhilarating and terrifying. You're not just launching a new business model; you're redefining how the world sees you. You may feel like you have to prove yourself all over again, even though your experience speaks for itself.

Here's what no one tells you: This discomfort is normal.

- You might feel like an imposter, despite your track record.
- You might second-guess every offer, every pricing decision, every pitch.
- You might feel vulnerable promoting yourself in a new way.

This isn't failure, it's growth. And your book can be one of your strongest allies during this time.

You don't need to be fully established to make an impact, you just need to be visible, intentional, and aligned with your purpose. As the first anchor in your ecosystem, your book helps you do exactly that.

Visibility Strategies for First-Time Entrepreneurs

If you're building a business from scratch, visibility can feel like the most daunting part. As we've talked about, you're not just selling a book but introducing a new version of yourself to the world. And that takes time, consistency, and trust. If you've set a strategic goal to start building visibility that feels authentic and aligned within your ecosystem, here are a few ways to achieve that:

> Want Help Mapping Out Your Business Model? Download a sample business plan tailored for author–entrepreneurs and designed to help you clarify your revenue goals, support systems, and pricing strategy. **promoteyourpurposebook.com/bonuses.**

- **Offer Free Talks or Workshops**
  Start by showing up where you already have trust. Reach out to associations, networking groups, or nonprofits you've been involved with and offer a free session related to your book's message. It's a great way to ease into public-facing work while adding value and building confidence.

- **Align Your Brand with Your Book**
  Use your book to update your LinkedIn headline, online bio, or website. The moment your book is out in the world it becomes a credential, so don't hide it! Let your book frame how others understand what you do now, not just what you've done in the past.

- **Create a Lead Capture and Nurture Funnel**
  Your book should lead somewhere. Set up a simple landing page with a free resource, such as a checklist, workbook, or guide that aligns with your book, and invite readers to sign up for your list. Then follow up with a short series of emails that introduce who you are, what you offer, and how they can work with you.

These visibility strategies don't require a massive audience or fancy tech. They just require clarity, consistency, and a willingness to show up. Remember your mindset shift: You're not "starting from scratch," you're "starting from experience." Your book gives you a strong platform to build on.

PROMOTE YOUR PURPOSE

Aligning Your Ecosystem

Turning your book into an ecosystem isn't about endless content creation, social media posts, email funnels, podcast tours, and bestseller campaigns. While these tactics absolutely have their place, they work only when built on the solid foundation of a strategy that reflects your actual needs. And that's what's often missing: alignment.

Whether among your purpose and vision, your goals, your business model, or your audience, each part of your marketing strategy and the role your book plays in it must be aligned. Forming your book's ecosystem is about building something that truly supports your purpose and goals. That's why I often recommend authors step back and ask themselves, "What am I trying to build, and how can this book help me get there?" From that clarity, everything else follows.

Authors frequently tell me they don't know how to "make the sale." They're great at showing up, speaking passionately, and networking with authenticity, but they get stuck turning those relationships into action. That's not a personal failing, it's a systems problem, and that problem is telling them their ecosystem needs to be rooted in their business model or purpose. As my friend and colleague Jennifer Brown, herself an established author and speaker with a 20-year track record running a successful consultancy, explained it during one of our recent conversations, the role of a thought leader is evolving: "The value proposition of thought leaders in the past was having all the answers. But now it's about making your questioning visible, and that becomes thought leadership. This shift is especially important for those of us navigating new identities after long careers. We don't need to present ourselves as finished products anymore. In fact, letting others witness our curiosity and growth can be one of the most powerful ways to build trust and invite people into our ecosystem."

Of course, a book and business model are only as strong as the systems that support them, including the ability to confidently sell what you offer, so we'll cover sales as a service in more detail later. For now, just know that this is where forming a small team becomes essential. Whether it's a marketing assistant, a speaking agent, or an operations-minded intern, you'll want to add someone to your ecosystem who can execute the vision while you stay focused on building relationships and delivering value.

Effective marketing is not about casting the widest net. It's about building meaningful connections with the people you're meant to serve and trusting that the rest will find something elsewhere that's more aligned for them.

PROMOTE YOUR PURPOSE

Relationships over Transactions: The Key to Authentic Book Marketing

One of the most powerful (and underutilized) truths in marketing is this: The clearer your strategy, the more your book resonates with the right people and quietly repels the wrong audience. And that's not a problem, it's the point.

Marketing a book isn't about numbers, it's about relationships. The most successful book promotions don't happen through aggressive advertising or obsessing over vanity metrics such as follower counts, and people don't buy books just because they exist. Successful book promotions happen when authors genuinely connect with their audiences, who buy books because they trust and resonate with the people behind them. This makes your book an extension of your expertise, perspective, and purpose, and being authentic in how you market these elements is key.

Your book and your marketing don't need to be for everyone. In fact, they shouldn't be. When you try to appeal to everyone, you dilute your voice and weaken your impact. But when you speak directly to the people who need what you offer—those who share your values, are ready for your message, and want to engage—you create magnetic alignment. The people who aren't a fit will self-select out, and that's a win. It saves everyone time, energy, and effort.

Effective marketing is not about casting the widest net. It's about building meaningful connections with the people you're meant to serve and trusting that the rest will find something elsewhere that's more aligned for them. So instead of viewing marketing as an exhausting list of tasks, I encourage you to see it as an opportunity to deepen your existing relationships and leverage adjacent networks. Who already knows and values your work? Who has access to the communities you want to reach? I call these people endorsers, borrowed audiences, and strategic partners, and they must be part of your ecosystem. They aren't just passive followers; they're people who understand your value and, when given the opportunity, will advocate for you. Your book is the tool that enables them to do that, and marketing then becomes about creating moments that allow those you've built relationships with to support your work, and in ways that benefit them too.

To truly activate this kind of support, you have to continue shifting from thinking about marketing as a transactional process to seeing it as a long-term relational practice. Marketing your book isn't just about who buys it but about who feels connected to your work and wants to share it.

An Invitation to Engagement, Not Follower Counts

Many authors believe marketing success is tied to the size of their social media following. But a massive audience does not guarantee sales. Authentic engagement does. And engagement is about creating conversations that lead to relationships, not about getting a million likes on a post. Instead of focusing on accumulating followers, shift your energy to one of these goals:

- Building genuine relationships with people who are interested in your topic
- Engaging in conversations rather than broadcasting promotions
- Offering value through insights, experiences, and real connections

Marketing works best when it's about reciprocity. If you engage meaningfully with others by responding to their questions, offering helpful advice, and showing up authentically, they're more likely to support you in return. Natalie Suppes, founder of S & S Creative, gave a presentation at PYP called "Social Media Engagement: Connecting with Your Ideal Readership," and she put it like this: "Posting is only half the work—relationship-building is the part that moves the needle. Commenting, saving posts, sending messages, showing up . . . that's where momentum comes from."

Think of your book as an invitation into your world, not just a standalone object to sell. By positioning yourself as someone with valuable knowledge and insights, your book becomes a natural extension of that credibility. People should see you as the expert first and the author second. This means showing up in conversations that relate to your book's topic, actively demonstrating your expertise instead of waiting for others to find it, and ensuring your book is visible across every touchpoint, including your website, email signature, LinkedIn bio, social media profiles, and any community platforms where you engage.

During a promotional event at PYP, Sam Lee, founder of IndeCollective, said, "Thought leadership isn't about attention. It's about reputation. Are you known for something? Do people understand what you stand for? When you lead with purpose, your audience doesn't just notice you, they trust you." This distinction is key when building an ecosystem around your book. Visibility alone won't grow your impact. It's about how clearly and consistently you communicate your values so that others can amplify your message, even when you're not in the room. Reputation is what earns trust, attracts aligned opportunities, and allows your book to serve as a signal of what you represent, not just content.

Leveraging Existing Communities and Word of Mouth

Many authors forget to tap into the communities they're already part of. Whether it's a professional network, a niche online group, or a local organization, engaging with your community can be one of the most effective ways to spread the word about your book.

When making this part of your Strategic Book Marketing Plan, ask yourself these questions:

- What communities am I already part of that align with my book's message?
- How can I contribute to these spaces in a way that feels natural and helpful?
- Who are the key people in these spaces I can build stronger relationships with?

The ultimate goal of relationship-based marketing is to have others talk about your book when you're not in the room. When people trust you and your work, they'll recommend your book to their networks.

Word of mouth is more powerful than any paid ad. Make it easy for others to share your book by providing clear messaging and accessible links. Encourage organic recommendations by asking people who express interest if they'd be willing to share your book with a friend or colleague. And don't forget to be generous in promoting others. When you support and celebrate fellow authors, they're often happy to return the favor.

Marketing as a Conversation, Not a Campaign

The most effective marketing doesn't feel like marketing. It feels like storytelling and connection-building. Whether it's social media, in-person events, or online communities, the best way to promote your book is to engage in conversations that naturally align with your expertise. Here are some ways to do this:

- ▸ Participate in discussions where your expertise is relevant. Answering questions, sharing insights, and helping others in online communities can make you a go-to resource.

- ▸ Find your people. Identify communities, networks, or influencers who care about what you care about. Engage with them authentically, not just as a means to an end.

- ▸ Show up consistently. Success isn't built on one viral moment but on steady, meaningful engagement over time.

People don't just buy books; they buy into the person behind them. Your energy, enthusiasm, and authenticity are your greatest marketing tools, and when you lead with them, your book becomes an invitation into your world. That's the power of treating your book as a central asset in a broader ecosystem. It can fuel your thought leadership, build trust with new audiences, and support your growth when it's aligned with your purpose and goals.

PROMOTE YOUR PURPOSE

TAKE ACTION
Map Your Author Ecosystem

Take a moment to ground your marketing strategy in clarity and purpose by asking yourself these questions. Using this space, a notebook, or the online workbook, write down your answers to these questions:

1. How does your book connect to each of the other three anchors of your ecosystem?

    ....

    ....

    ....

    ....

2. If you have an existing business, what is your business model? Are you high volume or low volume? Product-based or service-based? Do you rely on reach, relationships, or both?

    ....

    ....

    ....

    ....

3. Choose one or two ways your book can extend beyond the pages, whether through speaking, partnerships, consulting, or community-building.

    ....

    ....

TURN YOUR BOOK INTO AN ECOSYSTEM

....

....

....

4. Map out how your book connects to your bigger vision. Where does it fit in your client journey or revenue model?

....

....

....

....

....

Now, grab a blank sheet of paper, open a digital whiteboard, download a blank template from this book's website, or feel free to draw in this book. Draw a circle in the center and write your book title in it; this is the heart of your ecosystem. Add four spokes extending outward to represent the four anchors of your ecosystem (the book itself, your business, speaking, thought leadership). Under each anchor, jot down these points:

- ▸ How your book supports it
- ▸ One current or planned offering (e.g., service, talk, product, blog, event)
- ▸ One audience you're trying to reach
- ▸ One marketing activity you can do to deepen connection

This visual map will help you see how your book fits into the bigger picture and where to focus next to strengthen your impact, connection, and momentum.

PROMOTE YOUR PURPOSE

With clear goals and purpose-driven engagement, every marketing decision becomes easier and more effective.

> **PUT PURPOSE INTO PRACTICE** Choose one anchor of your ecosystem to strengthen over the next 30 days, whether it's the book itself, business, speaking, or thought leadership. Identify how your book currently supports that anchor and set one clear goal to deepen the connection. Take one simple action this week to move it forward.

CHAPTER 6
Know Your Reader, Know Your Buyer, Know Your Impact

You can write the best book in the world and position it within an ideal ecosystem, but if it doesn't reach the right people, it won't make the impact you intend. That's why defining your target reader and target buyer is foundational to both how you wrote your book and how you'll promote it.

One of the most common mistakes authors make is waiting until their book is done to figure out who it's for. Please avoid that pitfall. There's a reason this matters now, not later: The earlier you understand your reader, the better your book will resonate and drive your marketing strategy, giving you insight into where to show up and how to speak to your audience.

Since your book is part of a broader ecosystem, knowing your ideal reader isn't just about writing for them. It's about knowing how to reach them with services, products, or experiences that deepen their relationships with you.

Reader vs. Buyer

Are you marketing to your reader or to your buyer? Here's a powerful distinction: While they may sometimes be the same, the person who reads your book may not be the one who buys it.

Let's say your book is written for frontline employees, but you're selling it in bulk to HR teams or corporate training managers. In this case, your readers are the employees, but your buyers are the companies. This distinction is especially important for books that serve specific functions or audiences, such as business books used in workshops or training sessions and advocacy-oriented books leveraged by nonprofits or foundations. There are also books for younger readers that might be read and purchased by parents and educators but recommended or also bought by therapists. Both sides of the spectrum matter, but your marketing efforts need to be tailored to reach the buyers, not just the end readers.

As my cohost on the LinkedIn Live show *Unscripted with Ally & Jenn*, Ally Berthiaume often reminds our viewers, "The book ultimately leads your prospect or audience back to you in some capacity. What they're grasping for is what they're ready for on their journey, and once they're in your world you can nurture the next phase for them." This shift from thinking of a book as a product to thinking of it as a pathway can help you build both clarity and connection. It's not just about who reads your book but about what they do next.

Defining Your Target Reader

If you've done any branding or marketing work before, you may already be familiar with the concept of a target market. Through the lens of authorship, a target market is essential for meaningful engagement. You'll need to refine your audience beyond broad categories such as "women over 50," focusing on specific details including their professions, interests, and challenges. To gain clarity here, start by asking yourself these key questions:

- ▸ Where does my audience spend time?
- ▸ What podcasts do they listen to?
- ▸ What blogs, magazines, or media sources do they trust?
- ▸ Are they concentrated in particular geographic areas or among professional circles?

Answering these questions helps you target your efforts more effectively. For example, if your book is aimed at adoptive parents, connecting with workshops, therapy networks, and online support groups ensures your message reaches the right people. The more precisely you define your audience, the more effective your marketing strategy will be.

Let's break this down into four main categories:

KNOW YOUR READER, KNOW YOUR BUYER, KNOW YOUR IMPACT

1. Demographic Data

Demographic data is often the easiest to gather and includes these basics:

- Age range
- Gender identity
- Job title or industry
- Educational background
- Marital or parental status
- Generation (boomer, Gen X, millennial, etc.)

Why it matters: Different generations bring unique experiences and expectations that shape how they consume and connect with content. A Gen Z reader might engage through TikTok or interactive PDFs, while a Gen X buyer may prefer a print book or a podcast interview. These differences extend beyond format to include language, tone, and cultural references. A phrase that feels inclusive to one group may land as jargon, or even exclusionary, to another. Be intentional in how you describe your readers and the values you assume they hold. The goal isn't to market to everyone but to frame your message in a way that feels authentic and accessible to your audience. Generational and language awareness builds trust, deepens connection, and helps your book resonate across the spectrum of your intended readers.

2. Geographic Data

Data regarding the environment you'll tailor your marketing to may or may not be relevant for your book, but consider these points:

- Where do your readers live?
- Are they in urban, suburban, or rural settings?
- What region or country are they from?
- Do they speak or read English natively?

Why it matters: Regional context can affect references, tone, examples, or even the format of your outreach. For instance, audiobooks are more common in commuter-heavy areas, while printed books may be preferred in regions with limited internet access. Knowing your audience's environment helps you make informed decisions about distribution channels, event locations, pricing, and even the types of partnerships you pursue. If you're pitching to libraries, bookstores, or local media, geographic insights ensure you're targeting areas where your message is most likely to resonate.

3. Psychographic Data

In addition to physical data, it's essential to consider how your audience thinks:

- What are their values?
- What are their goals or fears?
- What keeps them up at night?
- What do they care most about in the world?

Why it matters: This is where real trust and loyalty are built. If your book supports a values-driven mission, knowing your audience's internal motivators allows you to craft messages that feel personal and empowering. For example, a book on leadership will land differently with readers motivated by legacy than it will with those seeking work–life balance. Understanding psychographics helps you choose the right tone, stories, and benefits to emphasize in your marketing.

4. Behavioral Data

Behavioral data covers the habits and preferences of those you're marketing to:

- Do they prefer digital content or physical books?
- What platforms do they engage with?
- Are they early adopters or cautious consumers?
- Are they likely to join a course or coaching program?

Why it matters: Knowing how your audience behaves helps you design marketing strategies that meet them where they already are. If your ideal readers prefer short-form video, a long blog post won't engage them. If they tend to purchase during launches or sales, plan your campaigns around those moments. Behavioral insights also help you tailor reader incentives, bonus content, and follow-up offers in ways that convert attention into action.

If you're not sure who your audience is yet, that's okay. While the ideal scenario is to have this mapped out while writing your book, many authors aren't completely clear on their reader or buyer until they begin marketing, and that's part of the process. The good news is that there are plenty of ways to find out:

- Ask your existing network. Survey your clients, email list, or social media followers.

- Use comparable titles. Look at Amazon and Goodreads reviews for books like yours. What do readers praise or criticize?

- Spy on competitors. Follow similar authors on LinkedIn, Instagram, or Substack. Who's engaging with their content?

- Leverage analytics. If you already produce content (e.g., blog posts, webinars, social media), look at who's engaging and what's performing best.

In a crowded
market, you
don't stand out
by being louder,
you stand out
by being clearer.

Differentiate Without Competing

Once you know who your ideal audience is, the next steps are defining what sets your message apart and evaluating how your marketing efforts will reach them. Are you engaging with your audience in the right places, or are there gaps you need to address?

Market differentiation isn't about being the loudest voice or the flashiest brand. It's about being unmistakably *you*. You have to connect with the people you're uniquely positioned to help, and that connection is your differentiator. In a crowded market, you don't stand out by being louder, you stand out by being clearer. The more specific you are about your values, methods, and lived experiences, the more trust you build with those you're marketing to. Readers want to know not just what you're saying but why it matters coming from you. That clarity is what creates staying power, and it's how your book becomes the one they remember.

Let's take a closer look at where you're showing up and where you might need to pivot. Ask yourself these questions:

- What do I see that others in my space often miss?
- What perspective, story, or approach do I bring that feels refreshingly different?
- What gap have I experienced or witnessed, and how does my book fill it?

When you can answer these questions, your book stops sounding like "just another take" and starts becoming the resource your audience has been waiting for. That clarity builds trust, and trust is what leads to visibility, opportunity, and impact.

Responding to Praise and Pain

As your book finds its way into the world, you'll likely encounter a mix of admiration, vulnerability, and projection. And when your message reaches the right people, the response can be deeper—and more emotional—than you might expect. This is part of being visible.

As an author, especially one who writes with vulnerability or purpose, you may find yourself at the receiving end of heartfelt praise, personal disclosures, or even unexpected trauma-sharing from your readers. Sometimes your most engaged readers aren't the people you initially expected but the ones who see themselves in your message. Even if you didn't write your book specifically for them, something you said might resonate deeply. That's the power of reader self-identification. Don't ignore those who raise their hands unexpectedly. When people feel seen, they're more likely to share your book, recommend it to others, or seek a deeper relationship with you and your work. Let their responses guide you. Your clearest audience may emerge not from data but from how real people respond.

This is a beautiful and complicated part of authorship. People will tell you your book changed their lives, and they may also tell you about the moment it mirrored a trauma they've never spoken aloud before. These are not just reactions to your book but are emotional invitations.

You don't have to accept every one.

It's more than okay to set boundaries around what you're willing or able to receive. You are not your readers' therapist or crisis counselor, and you are not obligated to carry their stories if doing so causes you harm. At the same time, it's important to be emotionally prepared, and you *can* respond with presence and compassion without overextending yourself. Here are a few gentle responses that create connection while protecting your emotional space:

- When someone offers praise, say something like, "Thank you so much for sharing that. It means a lot to know the book resonated with you."
- When someone shares something vulnerable or traumatic, say something like, "Thank you for trusting me with that. I'm honored the book made space for your story."

You don't need to fix anything, offer advice, or go deeper than you're comfortable with. These brief, intentional responses acknowledge the moment without pulling you into territory that feels unsafe or emotionally taxing.

Being clear about your own emotional capacity is an act of leadership. When you meet others' emotions with presence and boundaries, you model the very kind of transformation your book encourages.

Make Your Book a Natural Part of Your Work

If you're worried that promoting your book will feel like a second full-time job, you're not alone. But here's the truth: The most successful authors don't market their books as side projects. They weave them into the fabric of their existing work.

Your book should serve your mission, not distract from it. Ask yourself these questions:

- How can my book support the work I'm already doing?
- Where can I reference or share my book naturally, without needing a "campaign"?
- What conversations, presentations, or proposals already overlap with my message?

Whether you're coaching, consulting, training, or speaking, your book is a bridge. It helps your audience understand your approach, builds trust faster, and offers value before they ever work with you. Share it in proposals, client conversations, and presentations, and let it become a credibility asset, not a separate hustle.

When your book is integrated into the rhythms of your life or business, promotion becomes manageable and sustainable. Think of it simply as sharing what already aligns.

Who You're Really Reaching

When promoting your book, it helps to remember that you're not just speaking to one audience, you're speaking to three:

Audience	Role	Your Strategy
Readers	The people who will actually read your book	Focus on connection, transformation, and the value your book offers.
Buyers	The people making the purchase decision	Highlight practical benefits, credibility, and relevance to their needs.
Influencers	The people who can spread the word to others	Provide shareable content, clear talking points, and easy ways to amplify your message.

We'll talk more about influencers in part 2, but for now just know that each group plays a different yet essential role in your marketing success. When you tailor your outreach to meet them where they are, your book travels further—faster.

Books do not sell themselves. They find their way to the right people when you're clear on who those people are and how to reach them.

PROMOTE YOUR PURPOSE

Use this exercise to build clarity on who's your reader and who's your buyer so that you're prepared when it comes time to create your Strategic Book Marketing Plan. Thinking about this through the lens of promoting your book, answer these questions and write them down using this space, a notebook, or the online workbook:

1. Who is the ideal person/reader to reach?

....

....

....

2. What problem are they facing?

....

....

....

....

3. What transformation are you offering?

....

....

....

....

4. Who benefits most from reading your book?

....

....

....

....

....

....

5. Who is likely to *buy* the book, and why?

....

....

....

....

....

6. What makes your book different from others in your space? What's your unique edge?

....

....

....

....

....

....

Now ask yourself this: Is each of these the same person? If not, how will you tailor your marketing to both?

The process of promoting your book will give you even more data. Pay close attention to who reaches out for more help, which chapters or topics resonate most with your readers, and the feedback you're receiving through reviews or direct messages. These insights can guide your next steps, helping you refine your message, develop new offers, or identify opportunities for deeper engagement.

The clearer you are about your reader and buyer, the more confident you'll feel when it's time to launch. You'll know where to focus, how to position your message, and how to convert interest into action.

If you remember only one thing from this chapter, let it be this: Books do not sell themselves. They find their way to the right people when you're clear on who those people are and how to reach them. Let your readers shape your future offerings, and don't be afraid to pivot if a different audience begins to emerge.

PUT PURPOSE INTO PRACTICE

Map your target reader and buyer using the demographic, psychographic, geographic, and behavioral categories, then create one clear sentence that defines your audience.

Example: "My book is for mid-career nonprofit leaders seeking to make a greater impact through authentic leadership, and it's bought by HR teams and leadership program coordinators."

CHAPTER 7
Sell with Purpose, Serve with Confidence

It's time to talk about something that makes most authors squirm: *sales*. The word alone can bring up discomfort. For many aspiring entrepreneurs, selling feels sleazy or disingenuous, something they'd rather outsource to someone else. And yet here's the truth: If you want your book to create impact, you have to sell it. Whether you're promoting your book, pitching your services, or growing your visibility, sales are the bridges between your messages and the people who need them.

The same goes for *marketing*. If even the word makes you want to squirm a little, you're not alone. If you recall, I failed my first marketing class in college. It wasn't because I didn't care; it was because, at the time, the idea of marketing felt disconnected from anything meaningful. It felt transactional, not transformational. It took me years, and eventually a master's degree in integrated marketing communications, to understand that when done right, marketing is an act of service.

If you approach marketing as a way to serve your readers, share your ideas authentically, and create value for others, the entire experience becomes more organic, natural, and (dare I say it) even enjoyable. You don't have to be "good at marketing" in the traditional sense. You just have to be willing to show up, share your message, and trust that it will reach the people who need it most.

Marketing with Heart

Marketing isn't about shouting the loudest. It's about sharing your purpose with clarity and care. Start by asking yourself these questions:

- Where do I naturally love sharing ideas, helping people, or sparking conversations?
- How could I treat marketing as an extension of service rather than as self-promotion?
- What would marketing look like if it felt aligned with my values, not forced?

Service-driven marketing is not only more sustainable but also more magnetic. And here's something even more powerful to consider: Marketing is not a detour from your purpose but a way to fulfill it.

When you see your book as part of a larger mission within your ecosystem, every conversation, every post, every ask becomes a chance to include someone in the story you're building. Your readers want to feel part of something bigger. You're not promoting for the sake of attention; you're inviting your community to walk with you toward the change you're creating.

That's not hype. That's leadership.

Doubling Down vs. Watering Down: A Messaging Crossroads

Speaking of leadership, in moments of cultural or political tension, purpose-driven authors often face a difficult question: Should I double down on my values, or should I water them down to avoid backlash? For many of the authors we work with, this isn't a hypothetical but a very real dilemma.

The truth is that there's no neutral ground anymore. Your book either reinforces the status quo or calls for something different. But "doubling down" doesn't always mean being louder. It means being more strategic.

Dr. Steve Yacovelli, author of *Pride Leadership* and *Your Queer Career*, experienced an unexpected marketing moment when his book was listed among banned titles in a US Senate agriculture bill shortly after launch.

Rather than shrinking back, he leaned into the moment. We had a conversation about how to respond with purpose and presence, and we decided to celebrate the ban rather than fear it. Steve not only issued a press release proudly naming the censorship but used it as a launchpad to announce new scholarships for his leadership program, which is specifically for professionals in the agriculture sector who've been affected by legislation. The result? A burst of media attention, strong community support, and an authentic alignment of his book's values with real-world action.

Censorship is painful—and real—but it can also be an opportunity to double down on your purpose, amplify your message, and connect with readers who are ready to stand with you. As you consider how to market your book, ask yourself what you're willing to say boldly and how you can structure that message so more people are able to hear it. Reframe your message in a way that stays true to your purpose while widening your reach. Lead with impact, make your story accessible, and stay rooted in your values.

It's Not Self-Promotion, It's Community Engagement

For many purpose-driven authors, the word *promotion* brings up discomfort. It can feel like shouting into the void, asking for attention, or positioning yourself as "the expert." But here's a different way to think about it: Promotion isn't about putting yourself on a pedestal. It's about inviting people into something they care about.

We've talked about how important the right mindset is to building an impactful marketing strategy, so let's take it a step further. If the idea of "marketing your book" makes you cringe, try reframing it as "engaging your community." You're not asking people to buy something they don't need; you're offering a resource, an idea, a conversation that might help them or someone they know. So instead of thinking, *How can I promote this?* try asking these questions:

- ▸ Who already cares about this topic?
- ▸ Where are the people who need this message?
- ▸ What's the most generous way I can show up with value?

Marketing isn't about shouting the loudest. It's about sharing your purpose with clarity and care.

This shift from self-promotion to connection makes your outreach feel less forced and more human. It also builds trust, which is the true foundation of any meaningful marketing strategy.

What this looked like for me is that I started talking about this book before I finished the manuscript. I tested messages on social media, shared sneak peeks with authors, and even taught some of the content in workshops. Every time I did, I learned what resonated, and that shaped the final version of this book. If I had waited for perfection, none of that would've happened.

Visibility grows faster when you let people walk alongside you while you're building something.

You Can't Make an Impact Without Sales

This might sound obvious, but it's worth stating plainly: No matter how good your content is, your work will not make an impact unless you can sell it. You can be the most gifted coach, consultant, or speaker in your field, but if no one knows about your work or understands its value, your calendar will stay empty. This is a central idea in Michael Gerber's *The E-Myth*, a foundational book for entrepreneurs. Gerber explains that many small business owners are "technicians" at heart, experts in their craft, but they don't know how to run a business. They assume their skills will carry them, only to discover that sales, operations, marketing, and systems are what actually determine success.[4]

It's the same for author–entrepreneurs. Most authors I work with are deeply passionate, mission-driven people. They don't want to "sell" because they don't want to seem pushy or self-serving. But if you genuinely believe your book or service can help someone, why wouldn't you want to share it? Your book is a tool, and you are the salesperson. And that doesn't make you pushy, it makes you powerful.

Marketing gets easier when you shift your attention from yourself to your audience. Try this reframe: Instead of asking, "What will they think

---

4. Michael E. Gerber, *The E-Myth: Why Most Small Businesses Don't Work and What to Do About It* (HarperAudio, 2004), chapter 1, Audible.

of me?" try asking, "Who might need to hear this today?" When you lead with service, not self-consciousness, visibility becomes less about promoting yourself and more about helping someone take the next step.

Meet–Invite–Sell: A Simpler Sales Framework

Sales expert Allison Davis shared a brilliant, human-centered approach to sales in a workshop she hosted for PYP authors. Her "Meet–Invite–Sell" model breaks the sales process down into something intuitive and relational:

1. **Meet:** Show up and get to know your audience. Build rapport. Be curious.

2. **Invite:** Create an invitation for deeper conversation. Offer something of value, a workshop, a resource, a chat.

3. **Sell:** If the relationship feels aligned, make an offer. Don't just talk about your book or service but connect it to their needs.[5]

This approach flips the script on traditional, transactional sales tactics. Instead of pushing your message, you're creating space for connection. You're building trust.

This approach is particularly helpful in B2B spaces, where there's a growing trend: Companies are replacing traditional salespeople with subject matter experts. Why? Because people trust experts. They trust people who have lived experience, proven methods, and genuine passion for their work. Davis named something many authors struggle with in this arena: "vendor syndrome."[6] This is when subject matter experts like you and me show up to sales conversations as though we were order takers instead of the changemakers we are. We default to checking boxes instead of driving the conversation, we pitch services instead of uncovering needs, and we let our clients steer even when we know we can help guide them to better destinations.

---

5. Allison Davis, "Conference Best Practices for Small Business Owners," AllisonDavis.com, March 23, 2023, https://allison-davis.com/conference-best-practices-for-small-business-owners/.

6. Allison Davis, "Do You Have 'Vendor Syndrome?'" AllisonDavis.com, May 10, 2022, https://allison-davis.com/do-you-have-vendor-syndrome/#:~:text.

The antidote is to show up as the experts we already are. Ask better questions. Create tension not through conflict but through curiosity. Help our potential clients or readers imagine a better outcome, then guide them toward it. This is why author–entrepreneurs often make the best salespeople. We're not peddling a product; we're sharing a perspective. We're offering transformation.

But to do that effectively, we need to ask better questions. Here are three categories Davis suggests:

1. **Opening Questions**

   Build rapport and set the tone.
   - What made now the right time to talk about [your topic]?
   - What sparked your interest in [this challenge or goal]?

2. **Pain and Desire Questions**

   Uncover the deeper need.
   - What's not working for you right now?
   - What would a successful outcome look like?

3. **Peel-the-Onion Questions**

   Dig deeper. Challenge assumptions. Invite reflection.
   - What happens if you don't make this change?
   - Who else will be impacted if this stays the same?

When you shift from presenting solutions to asking meaningful questions, you become more than a vendor. You become a trusted guide.

Your Book Is Your Speaker Business Card

While we're on the topic of being a guide, if one of your goals is to actively build a speaking career, or if you're just testing the waters, your book is one of the most powerful tools in your tool kit. Event planners and conference organizers often weigh multiple qualified speakers for each opportunity. If everything else is equal—credentials, message, and delivery—the person with a book almost always gets the gig. Why? Because books are artifacts. They create instant credibility, offer something tangible to attendees, and demonstrate that an author has thought deeply about their message. In fact, many events buy books in bulk as takeaways for their audiences, which means your book can become both a teaching tool and a marketing asset.

Whether you're speaking for $5,000 or $50,000, your book is part of your pitch. You don't have to wait until you're "further along" to leverage it. The earlier you integrate authorship into your speaker brand, the faster you'll stand out. Remember: Visibility is not about vanity. It's about making it easy for the right people to find you.

Your Book and the Customer Journey

I've mentioned before that your book is not just a product but the beginning of a relationship. For many readers, discovering your book will be their first encounter with you. But if you're building a business, movement, or long-term message, it's essential to understand what happens after someone reads your book. That's where the customer journey comes in.

The customer journey is the path someone takes from discovering you to becoming an engaged, loyal part of your community. When you design your marketing with this journey in mind, it becomes easier, and by showing up with this purpose it becomes more strategic. Here's what that journey might look like:

- **Advocacy:** They become champions of your work. They leave reviews, invite you to speak, and bring new readers into your orbit.

- **Awareness:** They discover you through your book, podcast interviews, a blog post, or a referral.

- **Conversion:** They hire you, buy a product, join a program, or share your book with others.

- **Engagement:** They read more, attend a talk, reply to your email, or watch a video. They're leaning in.

- **Interest:** Something resonates. They follow you on social media, sign up for a resource, or browse your site.

- **Loyalty:** They return, recommend you, and trust your insights. You're no longer a stranger, you're a guide.

Too often, authors stop at the "Buy my book" stage. But your real impact, influence, and income often live in the layers that come after. When you start to map this journey intentionally, your book becomes the most powerful invitation you have. You don't need a complicated funnel; you just need clarity. When you understand how your book fits into your ecosystem, you see the bigger picture, and that allows you to serve more powerfully and sell with more confidence.

Remember: Your message doesn't have to be louder than someone else's, it just has to be clearer. Go back to what makes your book different. That's your hook.

Your book is the beginning of the conversation, not the end.

As you think about selling with purpose, don't stop at one post or one podcast. Think about how your book connects to the next meaningful step in your ecosystem and how you can continue to show up for your audience every step of the way. That starts with understanding the path your reader takes from discovering your book to becoming a part of your greater mission. Record your thoughts either here, in a notebook, or by accessing the online workbook, and keep your answers with you.

Step 1: Reflect on Your Ecosystem

Think about how someone first encounters your work. Is it through a podcast, blog post, speaking engagement, workshop, or personal referral? Note that here.

....
....
....
....
....
....
....
....
....
....

Step 2: Identify the Next Step

Your book is often the beginning of a relationship, not the end. What small, meaningful step can a reader take after finishing your book that draws them closer to your work?

....

....

....

....

Step 3: Design the Invitation

What does it look like to warmly and clearly invite people into your world, whether that's through a newsletter, consultation, course, or community?

....

....

....

....

Step 4: Build the Relationship

Marketing doesn't stop once someone says yes. How will you stay connected and keep delivering value over time?

....

....

....

....

SELL WITH PURPOSE, SERVE WITH CONFIDENCE

Selling, when done right, is not about convincing but about connecting. So reframe how you think about visibility and promotion: Sales aren't about applying pressure; they're about opening up possibilities. Marketing isn't about shouting the loudest; it's about telling a meaningful story. And showing up as an author doesn't require perfection; it simply requires presence. Your book is the beginning of the conversation, not the end.

> **PUT PURPOSE INTO PRACTICE**
>
> Which part of the Meet-Invite-Sell framework feels most natural to you? Which part feels hardest? Write one small actionable step to build your sales confidence this week, whether it's reaching out to a past client or practicing your pitch aloud.

STRATEGIC READINESS
What You'll Need for the ASPEN Method

Before diving into part 2 and creating your Strategic Book Marketing Plan using the ASPEN Method, let's take a moment to reflect and prepare. This premarketing checklist gathers all the foundational elements you've built so far from part 1. Reflect on each one and realign where needed so you can move forward with intention.

Core Foundations

- [ ] **Your Purpose / Why (chapter 1)**
  The reason behind your book and the change you hope to create
- [ ] **Your Vision (chapter 1)**
  What success looks like for you personally, professionally, and in your community
- [ ] **Your Intended Impact (chapter 1)**
  The transformation you want your readers (and the world) to experience because of your book
- [ ] **Your Strategic SMART Goals (chapter 2)**
  Marketing goals that are specific, measurable, attainable, realistic, and timely
- [ ] **Your Book Description (chapter 2)**
  A reader-facing book description that aligns with your message, audience, and goals
- [ ] **Your Perspective on Marketing (chapter 3)**
  Your personal viewpoint on marketing that will shape how you approach visibility, engagement, and consistency
- [ ] **Your Tagline (chapter 3)**
  A short, powerful phrase that communicates what you do, who you help, and the transformation you offer

Support Systems and Safety Nets

- [ ] **Your Marketing Support Team (chapter 4)**
  The peers, professionals, or partners who will help you execute your plan
- [ ] **Your Accountability Partner(s) (chapter 4)**
  One or more people who will support you in staying on track and aligned with your goals
- [ ] **Your Structured Backup Plans (chapter 4)**
  Your proactive IF/THEN responses for when things don't go according to plan

Strategic Alignment

- [ ] **Your Ecosystem Map (chapter 5)**
  A visual or written overview of how your book connects to your services, offerings, and thought leadership
- [ ] **Your Target Reader and Buyer Profiles (chapter 6)**
  A clear understanding of the demographics, geographics, psychographics, and behavioral patterns of those you'll be marketing to
- [ ] **Your New Sales Mindset (chapter 7)**
  The internal shift that reframes marketing as service, not self-promotion
- [ ] **Your Customers' Journey (chapter 7)**
  How your audience first encounters your work and the steps they'll take to engage more deeply

If you haven't downloaded the online workbook yet, now's the time. As you move into part 2 and start building your Strategic Book Marketing Plan, having everything in one place will make the process easier and more effective. Visit promoteyourpurposebook.com/bonuses to get your copy and stay organized as you take action.

PART 2: THE ASPEN METHOD

You've made it to the heart of the journey, where strategy meets action.

In the following chapters, I'll show you how to approach your book promotion in a way that feels intentional and achievable. We'll dive into the ASPEN Method framework, a structured yet flexible approach to marketing your book with clarity and confidence using five pillars that will help you attract the right readers, build momentum, and create lasting impact:

ASSESS
Evaluate your audience, current marketing efforts, and personal strengths.

STRATEGIZE
Develop a plan that includes clear calls to action, pre-order strategies, and alignment with a cause.

PLAN
Identify potential buyers and influencers, determine outreach strategies, and repurpose your existing content.

EXECUTE
Prioritize high-impact activities that align with your time, budget, and energy.

NURTURE
Sustain engagement through email marketing, speaking opportunities, and ongoing community-building.

Whether you're in the early brainstorming phase, halfway through your promotional strategies, or holding your book marketing plan in your hands and wondering what to do next, part 2 is built to support you. And whether your goal is to sustain long-term visibility, secure bulk sales, book speaking engagements, or integrate your book into your broader ecosystem, this framework is designed to meet you where you are. It ensures that every marketing effort you make is intentional, aligned with your goals, and most of all, manageable.

Consider this your companion, not a checklist. Marketing a book is no small feat, and this is where mindset plays a crucial role, especially for self-published authors who are navigating a system that still favors traditional pathways.

The ASPEN Method isn't about doing everything at once. Instead, think of it as a "Pick Your Path" guide. Not all of you will start from the same place or share the same goals, so you'll see suggestions throughout for where you might want to go next depending on your unique circumstances. Here's how to move through part 2 based on what you've already done or what you're ready for next:

- ▶ If you're ready to roll up your sleeves and start assessing your platform, proceed to chapter 8.

- ▶ If you've already completed a recent assessment of your platform and know where you want to focus, skip to chapter 9 to start building your strategy.

- ▶ If you've already developed a marketing strategy and are ready to plan your marketing activities, skip to chapter 10.

PART 2: THE ASPEN METHOD

- ▶ If your marketing strategy is already mapped out, skip to chapter 11 to start taking action and executing your plan.

- ▶ If you've already executed your marketing plan and are now looking to nurture it, skip to chapter 12.

- ▶ If you've already determined how you'll nurture your book's impact, skip to appendix A, where you'll find Your Book Marketing Essentials Checklist.

Wherever you are right now, whether enthusiastic, unsure, scattered, or cautiously optimistic, this framework is here to help you build a marketing strategy that not only works but feels good while doing it.

Each of the following chapters explores one pillar of the ASPEN Method, and each step is placed in sequential order because each builds upon the last to create a marketing approach that's intentional and aligned. That said, feel free to flip to what's most relevant to you at the stage you're in.

Since this book is designed to be intentional, evergreen, and sustainable, these resources live on the book's website, allowing you to view them regularly as new tools, tactics, and trends emerge so that the guidance remains relevant over time.

To make the most out of part 2, keep a notebook handy, have this book's website open in a new browser, and/or download the online companion workbook to capture your thoughts, breakthroughs, and plans. Star the action items that feel most relevant right now. Don't worry about doing it all, as this is about building a strategy that works for you. All you have to do is start.

ASSESS

CHAPTER 8: Assess Your Platform, Purpose, and Possibilities

PICK YOUR PATH — *If you've already completed a recent assessment of your platform and know where you want to focus, skip to chapter 9 to start building your strategy.*

Before you begin mapping your journey, you need to assess the landscape you've already built. So in this chapter, we're going to explore the Assess phase of the ASPEN Method.

Assessing provides clarity on where you stand, which in turn helps you identify gaps before investing time or money into ineffective strategies. The goal is to take inventory of your existing efforts and determine the best ways to reach your target audience. By understanding what's already in place, you can align your marketing approaches with what feels sustainable and impactful.

We're going to cover six key areas of assessment:

1. Your book's position in the market
2. Your current marketing activities
3. Your existing content
4. Your personal brand and presence
5. Competitor and industry trends
6. The alignment between your marketing strategies and your strengths

PROMOTE YOUR PURPOSE

This phase lays the foundation for a strategic and intentional plan, ensuring your efforts are focused on the most effective activities moving forward. Think of this chapter as your marketing GPS—it's how you'll chart the clearest route to your goals.

Positioning Your Book

Before you take the first step in the Assess phase, it's essential to determine your book's positioning. For many authors, particularly those from underrecognized communities, self-publishing isn't a fallback plan but the only way to get their stories into the world. Yet the publishing industry continues to reinforce a hierarchy in which traditionally published books are treated as more legitimate. Authors working at the intersection of activism, identity, or cultural change often find themselves locked out of mainstream coverage, awards, or distribution regardless of the quality of their work. As one pair of authors shared with me, "We've built a grassroots following and sold books through community networks, but the lack of equitable support from major platforms has been a recurring struggle."

This is why positioning matters. Whether you self-publish, go independent, work with a hybrid publisher, or use a small press, you can build credibility, visibility, and influence without waiting for validation from industry gatekeepers.

Here's a checklist to help you assess or refine your book's professional positioning, whether you're starting from scratch or fine-tuning what you've already built:

- [ ] **Invest in Publisher-Quality Cover Art and Interior Design**

    Work with experienced professionals who understand your genre. A polished cover design and interior layout help your book stand out and feel credible.

- [ ] **Register an Imprint Name**

    An imprint is your publishing brand name, which appears instead of self-publishing distribution platforms such as Amazon KDP or IngramSpark. Register it when purchasing your ISBNs to strengthen your professional image.

☐ **Purchase Your ISBNs Directly from Bowker**

Each format of your book needs its own ISBN. Buying from Bowker gives you full ownership and control.

☐ **Distribute via IngramSpark**

IngramSpark distribution allows bookstores, libraries, and retailers to order your book. It also signals to the industry that your book is widely available and accessible.

☐ **Secure Professional Editorial Reviews**

Reviews from sources such as Kirkus, Clarion, or BlueInk add credibility and help with visibility. Consider newer review services that support indie authors too.

☐ **Submit to Indie-Friendly Award Programs**

Awards offer visibility and third-party validation. Focus on those that welcome self, indie, or hybrid published books.

☐ **Leverage Endorsements from Respected Voices**

Endorsements from experts or leaders in your field can help build trust. Use them on your book cover, website, and marketing materials.

☐ **Include a Compelling Media Kit**

Include your bio, book summary, talking points, and highlights. A clear media kit helps podcasts, media outlets, and event hosts promote your work with ease.

Your voice is valid. Your book is worthy. And your message matters—even if you're building it outside the gates.

> Your voice is valid. Your book is worthy. And your message matters—even if you're building it outside the gates.

Your Current Marketing Activities

The first step of developing any book marketing plan is crucial: Assess what you're already doing. This means taking inventory of your current marketing efforts to see what's working and what isn't.

Grab a piece of paper, open a spreadsheet, or go to the online workbook and identify the platforms you're using, including any social media, newsletters, networking groups, or speaking engagements. Consider their effectiveness and your level of engagement:

- How many people are connected to you?
- How often do you interact with them?
- What do you like about this activity?
- What do you dislike about this activity?

Run through this exercise for all your existing marketing efforts to get a clear picture of what's working and feels aligned.

If you dislike certain marketing efforts, sustaining them long-term will be a challenge. If social media doesn't energize you, consider alternative strategies that better suit your strengths. Email marketing allows for direct engagement with your audience; guest appearances on podcasts position you as an expert; and tapping into existing listener bases, attending networking events, or contributing to industry newsletters helps you build credibility and connections. If a marketing channel is outdated or ineffective, such as a Facebook page with little engagement, removing it can free up time for more impactful activities.

The key is to focus on strategies that are not only effective but also aligned with your goals, audience, and resources. One author I worked with, who was writing a book about life transitions and career changes, was offered an advertising package from a large media company: on-air radio ads promoting her book and services for $4,000 per month. While it sounded

> Looking for consistent support and accountability? Explore PYP's marketing groups and connect with fellow authors who are promoting their books with purpose—visit **promoteyourpurposebook.com/bonuses**.

impressive—wide reach, frequent airtime, and a mainstream platform—when we evaluated the numbers and audience fit, it became clear she wouldn't recoup that investment through book sales alone. Even more importantly, the listening audience didn't closely align with her target readers. After a thoughtful conversation, she chose to walk away.

The lesson? Just because a strategy seems high profile doesn't mean it's high impact. It's better to invest in marketing that's purposeful, targeted, and financially sustainable.

Your Existing Content

Once you've reviewed your marketing efforts, it's time to assess what content you already have and leverage it, which is a significant part of marketing. Many authors think they need to create new material from scratch, but chances are you have valuable content you can repurpose into fresh formats. By doing so, you can maximize your reach while saving time and effort.

Before creating new materials, take inventory of your existing content to see what you can repurpose:

- **Blog Posts**

    A well-performing blog post can be adapted into a LinkedIn article, a social media post, or an email newsletter. Even shorter posts can become quote cards or pulled into a series.

- **Podcasts**

    A podcast discussion can be transcribed into a written article or summarized in a video format or quote graphics. You can also pitch similar episodes to other shows.

- **Speeches, Presentations, or Workshops**

    Talks you've delivered (even informally) can be broken into smaller lessons or tip lists and turned into blog posts or an email series. (For more information on TEDx and signature talks, see appendix B.)

- **Online Course Material**

    If you've ever created a training, webinar, or self-guided course, even if it's simple, those outlines and modules can be repackaged into lead magnets, video clips, or articles that tie back to your book's themes.

- **Website Articles**

    Revisit your site's archive. Older articles can be updated with fresh stats or calls to action and then reused on platforms such as Medium, Substack, or LinkedIn.

- **Newsletters**

    Browse your past email campaigns. Many newsletters include storytelling, insights, or curated resources that can be bundled into ebooks, mini-series, or content for future marketing.

- **Coaching Sessions**

    If you lead or participate in coaching calls, consider recording and transcribing them (with permission). These sessions often contain valuable insights, language, and real-world examples that can be repurposed into blog posts, articles, or thought leadership pieces for various platforms. I regularly use this approach to turn coaching moments into reflective Substack essays that resonate with a wider audience. You can view them at promoteyourpurpose.substack.com.

Repurposing content saves time and expands your reach across different platforms. By strategically reusing content, you can maximize exposure and engagement without constantly creating from scratch.

This is where I find the power of AI to be an incredible marketing tool. Once upon a time you needed to hire a virtual assistant or a marketing admin of some kind to help you modify or adapt past material into something new. But now you can use AI to help you with these tasks. If you have a well-performing blog post on your website, for instance, but do not want to get dinged in the search engines for creating duplicate content, put it into AI

> To see AI's impact on thought leadership, visit **promoteyourpurposebook.com/bonuses** and access my joint resource with Jennifer Brown.

and ask it to help you rewrite for a different medium, outlet, or format, then modify from there. Ensure the new creation is in your voice, style, and tone, however, or your audience will very quickly see you're using AI, which may come across as disingenuous.

How One Author Found Her Marketing Momentum

One of my clients, a trauma-informed leadership coach, came to me feeling completely overwhelmed by marketing. She didn't have an email list, her blog had only ten posts, and she felt like she was "behind" on everything. But during our assessment, we discovered that one of her early blog posts had been reshared by a major nonprofit, and that single post had already earned her credibility in her niche. We just hadn't noticed it yet.

To get her from overwhelmed to aligned, we built her launch strategy around that one piece of content. She used it to reconnect with her audience on LinkedIn, pitch to three organizations that had shared it, and secure speaking opportunities at all three. As a result, she landed 200 book pre-orders and set the tone for her brand as a thought leader—all without creating anything new, just aligning with what was already working.

What This Looked Like for Me

Repurposing existing content has been one of the most effective ways I've streamlined my book-writing process while maximizing the value of content I've already created. In *Publish Your Purpose*, I leveraged blog posts, blueprints, and online courses to enrich my book while keeping readers engaged across multiple platforms.

One of the best examples of this is PYP's Book Cost Blueprint, a downloadable PDF available on our website.[7] This guide covers myths about publishing costs, different publishing models, and the financial

---

7. https://publishyourpurpose.com/book-cost-blueprint-optin/.

investment authors need to consider. Rather than creating entirely new content, I incorporated much of this material into chapter 16, "Your Publishing Cost," revising it slightly to better fit a book format while keeping about 95 percent of the content the same. I also included a call to action at the end of the chapter, directing readers back to my website to download the full blueprint. This way they could access the material in a format that worked best for them while also engaging further with my brand.

I also repurposed several blog posts into book chapters. For instance, my blog post "Crowdfunding for Authors: Raise Funds for Your Book" became nearly identical to a section in chapter 16 titled "Five Tips on Crowdfunding for Authors." Since the content was already well-researched and fully developed, it made sense to integrate it without needing to rewrite everything from scratch. By doing this, I created what I like to call a circular loop, bringing previously created content into the book while also guiding readers back to those external resources. This approach keeps people engaged beyond the pages of my books, allowing them to continue learning and connecting with me in different ways.

If you've already created content, whether in blog posts, podcasts, online courses, or speeches, you don't have to start your marketing materials from scratch. Instead, look at your book's outline and identify where your existing content aligns with your marketing goals and messages. This will not only save you time but also help you create a more cohesive and engaging experience for your readers.

> Want to see a real-life example of content repurposing in action? In a short video, I walk you through exactly how I transformed blog posts, blueprints, and courses into book chapters without starting from scratch. Watch here: **promoteyourpurposebook.com/bonuses**.

> A strong personal brand builds trust and recognition, making it easier for people to connect with and remember you.

Your Personal Brand and Presence

Your personal brand is how you show up in the world and how people perceive you, so it should align with your book, business, and overall promotional messages. A strong personal brand builds trust and recognition, making it easier for people to connect with and remember you. If your brand isn't clearly defined, it's time to assess how you present yourself across platforms.

Branding is more than just visuals such as colors and logos. It includes your tone, messaging, and core strengths. Are you an engaging speaker, a skilled storyteller, or an empathetic listener? Those strengths should be reflected in how you market yourself and your book. Your branding must also be consistent across different platforms; if it's not, audiences may struggle to understand what you stand for. So ensure your messaging, appearance, and communication style are cohesive across your website, social media, and professional interactions.

To assess and strengthen your personal brand, follow these steps:

1. **Define Your Brand's Core Identity**
   Start by identifying what your personal brand stands for and ensure it aligns with your book, business, and overall message. Ask yourself, "What do I want people to think of when they hear my name?" Having a clear vision will guide all your branding efforts.

2. **Assess Consistency Across Platforms**
   Review your website, social media, and marketing materials to check for alignment in messaging, visuals, and tone. If your platforms present conflicting versions of you, refine them to create a unified and recognizable presence.

3. **Gather External Feedback**
   Look through past emails, testimonials, and referrals to find patterns in how others describe you. Ask colleagues, friends, or clients to share three words they associate with you. Also pay attention to how people introduce you in emails because these introductions often reflect your strongest traits and help shape your brand identity.

4. **Identify Your Unique Strengths (Your Superpowers)**

   Consider what people frequently compliment you on and what skills or qualities make you stand out. Your personal brand should highlight these strengths in a way that resonates with your audience. If you're known for delivering high-quality work, being a visionary thinker, or having a unique storytelling ability, make sure those attributes are reflected in your brand.

5. **Optimize Your Digital Presence**

   During an internal training for PYP authors called "How to Build Your Author Brand," Kree Pandey Aryal, founder of OTVO Digital, explained, "In a marketplace flooded with books, your digital presence must rise to the level of the message you're sharing." This means your website should reflect the same thoughtfulness, intention, and clarity as your writing, especially because it's often the first impression your audience will have of you. Optimize your digital presence by securing a domain name that aligns with your name or expertise, such as YourName.com or YourNameAuthor.com. If you already have a business website, consider adding a dedicated personal brand page. Be sure to use a professional logo and a consistent color scheme and typography to enhance your brand recognition and credibility.

6. **Refine Your Messaging and Visual Identity**

   Align your brand's tone with your personality, whether that's approachable, bold, strategic, or inspiring. Ensure your website imagery, headshots, and content reflect your authentic self. If needed, consult a branding expert to create a cohesive and professional brand identity.

7. **Leverage Strategic Brand Cohesion**

   If you run multiple business ventures, develop a branding system that ties them together. Decide whether you want a single, unified brand or separate but complementary brands. Again, maintain consistency in colors, fonts, and themes across your book, website, and promotional materials to reinforce brand recognition. For example, this is what my personal brand logo looks like compared with the PYP logo; you can clearly see the uniformity through the typography, and if you look on our website you can see the cohesion of colors as well:

8. **Make Your Brand Easily Discoverable**

    To simplify navigation for your audience, use redirects such as forwarding YourName.com to your main business website. Ensure all digital assets, from social media profiles to email signatures, link back to a central hub. If you have multiple books or projects, connect them under a single, recognizable brand to avoid diluting your audience's attention.

9. **Evolve and Adapt as Needed**

    Your personal brand should grow with you, so periodically reassess how you're showing up in the world. Seek feedback, update visuals, and refine your messaging as your goals evolve. A well-crafted and adaptable personal brand builds trust, credibility, and lasting impact, making it easier for people to connect with and remember you.

By following these steps, you'll create a clear, compelling, and cohesive personal brand that strengthens your book, business, and visibility while ensuring long-term recognition and success.

> Want to define and strengthen your personal brand so it aligns with your book, business, and overall message? In this short video and guided exercise, I'll walk you through how to uncover what your brand stands for, identify your unique strengths, and ensure your visuals and messaging are cohesive across platforms. I'll also give you recommendations for trusted providers who can help you execute this work. Watch here: **promoteyourpurposebook.com/bonuses**.

Competitor and Industry Trends

Now that you've defined your personal brand and ensured consistency across platforms, it's time to leverage that clarity in your marketing efforts. The key to a successful and sustainable book marketing plan is choosing methods that align with your strengths, because if you dislike a certain approach, staying consistent will be a struggle.

Understanding what similar authors are doing can provide valuable insights into where to focus your efforts, so research authors in your niche and observe how they engage their audience. For example, if your book targets therapists, identify where they network and seek information. Are they active in professional associations, specific conferences, or industry-specific online groups?

Pick three authors in your niche and analyze their marketing efforts:

- What platforms do they prioritize?
- What kind of content gets the most engagement?
- Make a note of trends that align with your strengths and consider testing similar strategies.

Understanding where your audience already congregates allows you to position yourself in those spaces rather than trying to build an audience from scratch. By staying informed on trends and best practices in your field, you can refine your marketing strategies and connect with your ideal audience more effectively.

Aligning Your Marketing with Your Strengths

The key to successful marketing is leaning into what feels authentic rather than forcing strategies that don't fit. Many experts may tell you that you need to be on every platform, but spreading yourself too thin can be counterproductive. Marketing should be built around what feels natural to you. If you dislike a particular approach, forcing yourself to do it will drain your energy and make consistency difficult. Instead, focus on methods that align with your strengths, then choose one or two core tactics you enjoy and commit to them fully. If social media feels overwhelming, don't rely on it as your primary marketing tool. If you prefer in-person interactions, then prioritize conferences, networking events, and speaking engagements. If writing is your strength, then focus on email newsletters, blogs, and guest articles.

This is where a SWOT analysis can be especially helpful. It's a classic business tool that helps you take a strategic inventory of your current landscape, and it breaks down like this:

- **Strengths:** internal assets, skills, or qualities working in your favor
- **Weaknesses:** internal challenges or gaps that may be holding you back
- **Opportunities:** external trends, relationships, or emerging possibilities you can leverage
- **Threats:** external risks or market shifts that could interfere with your success

This simple framework gives you a strategic snapshot that can shape your book marketing, inform your business plan, or guide your next creative project.

Whether you need one SWOT for your business and one for your book depends on your book's positioning. If your book is closely tied to your business, platform, or thought leadership, a single SWOT analysis can cover both; your book is part of your larger ecosystem, so it's useful to look at your author platform and business goals through a unified lens.

> Sustainable marketing honors your preferences, your pace, and your energy. The goal isn't to do it all but to consistently do what works *for you*.

However, if your book stands apart from your business, such as it targeting a completely different audience, you may want to complete two separate SWOTs or use different colors or labels to distinguish them.

To illustrate how a single SWOT can inform both book marketing and business strategies, here's a real-world example from my own platform.

STRENGTHS	WEAKNESSES
✓ Strong industry credibility and publishing expertise ✓ Established email list and trusted brand (Publish Your Purpose) ✓ Highly aligned, values-driven audience	✓ Limited time for 1:1 sales or outreach ✓ Difficulty translating expertise into marketable offers ✓ Occasionally underprice or over give in early-stage offers
OPPORTUNITIES	**THREATS**
✓ Expand demand for inclusive, purpose-driven publishing ✓ Strategic partnerships and speaking engagements ✓ Leveraging book (*Promote Your Purpose*) to open new revenue streams	✓ AI tools creating a flood of generic content in the market ✓ Political/social shifts may impact visibility or perceived "controversy" in inclusive messaging ✓ Rising costs for vendors and services affecting profit margins

Assessing your marketing isn't just about reviewing what already exists. It's also about uncovering what actually works for you. Sustainable marketing honors your preferences, your pace, and your energy. The goal isn't to do it all but to consistently do what works *for you*. When you take an honest inventory of your book's positioning, your current marketing activities, your existing content, your brand, trends in the industry, and your strengths, you create the foundation for a marketing approach that's both authentic and sustainable.

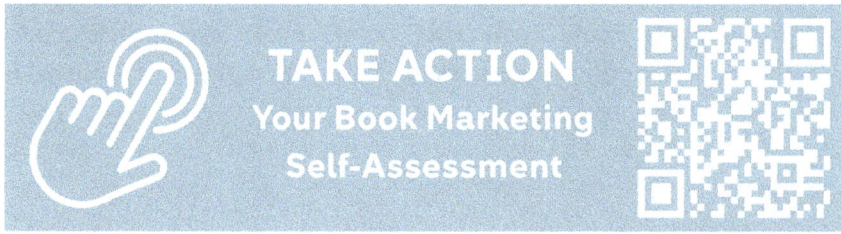

Let's pull it all together. Before you move into the next phase of the ASPEN Method, take a moment to step back and assess where you are right now. These reflective exercises are designed to help you clarify your foundation, uncover blind spots, and identify opportunities to strengthen your overall approach to book marketing. Use this space, your own notebook, or the online workbook to jot down your insights and next steps.

Remember: This is just the first step of the ASPEN Method. Take the time to thoroughly assess where you are and what you have before moving on.

Your Mini Marketing Audit

Use the following quick prompts to run a self-assessment of your current marketing setup:

What is your book's professional positioning, and how can you use it to build credibility, visibility, and influence?

....

....

....

Where are you showing up? Where are you invisible? Are you active where your audience actually spends time or are there missed opportunities?

....

....

PROMOTE YOUR PURPOSE

What content are you sitting on that you haven't yet leveraged? Dig into past blog posts, webinars, courses, or slide decks. There's gold in your archives.

....
....
....
....

What three adjectives best describe your brand? Do they match how others see you? Cross-check your brand perception with how others introduce or describe you.

....
....
....
....

What competitor or industry trends do you see in your niche, and how could you focus your marketing efforts on positioning yourself in those spaces to provide valuable insights and engage your audience?

....
....
....
....

Your Author SWOT Analysis

Now that you've completed your mini audit, you have a clearer sense of what's working in your marketing and where you may want to pivot. This is the perfect moment to pull it all together with a SWOT analysis. Use the following prompts to guide your own analysis on the following page.

STRENGTHS	WEAKNESSES
✓ What do I do well as an author, speaker, or business owner? ✓ What platforms or content formats already work for me? ✓ What makes my voice, brand, or message unique?	✓ Where do I lack skills, clarity, or consistency? ✓ What platforms or strategies drain me or fall flat? ✓ What feedback have I received that points to areas of improvement?
OPPORTUNITIES	**THREATS**
✓ What partnerships, trends, or platforms could help me grow? ✓ What untapped audiences or services align with my message? ✓ What's changing in my space that I could take advantage of?	✓ What industry trends, tech changes, or external challenges could impact my reach or sales? ✓ What distractions or resource limitations could stall my momentum? ✓ Where might I be vulnerable if I don't adapt or evolve?

Now, jot down your analysis in a notebook or access the editable version in the online workbook.

STRENGTHS	WEAKNESSES

OPPORTUNITIES	THREATS

The goal of this assessment isn't just to see what's working. It's to recognize what needs to shift. Whether that means pivoting your platform, refreshing your messaging, or realigning your goals, this clarity sets you up to take intentional action and is a powerful step toward marketing with clarity and confidence. It helps you see the big picture, what you're already doing well, where you can grow, and how to navigate the external landscape around your book and business.

ASSESS YOUR PLATFORM, PURPOSE, AND POSSIBILITIES

Keep your SWOT as a living document you revisit and refine over time. As your goals evolve, your strengths, challenges, and opportunities will evolve too.

Now that you've assessed your assets and analyzed your SWOTs, it's time to move forward with focus. Review your notes and choose one area where you'll make a meaningful change this week. Maybe it's retiring a platform that drains you, repurposing a blog post for a new audience, or refreshing your brand message for clarity. Let intention lead the way.

PUT PURPOSE INTO PRACTICE

Before you start building momentum, make sure you're pointed in the right direction. What surprised you in your SWOT analysis? What strengths or blind spots did you uncover?

STRATEGIZE

CHAPTER 9: Strategize Your Visibility and Audience Growth

PICK YOUR PATH

If you've already developed a marketing strategy and are ready to plan your marketing activities, skip to chapter 10.

In the last chapter, you assessed your platform, purpose, and possibilities, and you identified where you're already gaining traction (strengths and opportunities) and where you need to pivot (weaknesses and threats). Now it's time to build momentum with the Strategize phase.

Strategy isn't about doing everything. It's about doing the right things, in the right order, in the right way. You don't have to build fast to build effectively. A slow, deep foundation built on clarity, alignment, and purpose often outlasts the flashiest launch.

In this chapter, we will explore four key elements of your marketing strategy:

- **Creating Strategic Calls to Action**

  Ensure your book directs readers toward deeper engagement, whether through email sign-ups, downloads, speaking inquiries, or other methods.

- **Aligning with a Cause**

  Use cause marketing to create deeper connections and position your book as part of something bigger.

- **Expanding Your Reach Through Strategic Partnerships**

  Collaborate with organizations, companies, or key individuals to amplify your visibility, increase credibility, and create bulk sales opportunities.

- **Devising Your Book Launch and Pre-Order Strategies**

  Build momentum through intentional campaigns that increase visibility, strengthen relationships, and support long-term goals.

This phase is about intentionality. Rather than relying on scattered efforts, you'll develop a strategy that connects your book to larger opportunities, revenue streams, and long-term engagement. Whether you're launching your book, growing your business, or establishing yourself as a thought leader, this chapter will help you strategize a book marketing plan that boosts your visibility and aligns with your unique strengths and goals.

Strategic Calls to Action: Engaging Readers Beyond Your Book

One of the biggest challenges authors face is that when a book is sold, they have no way of knowing who bought it. Unlike email marketing or direct sales when you collect valuable audience insights, book sales through retailers such as Amazon, Barnes & Noble, or your local independent bookstore provide only sales numbers, not customer details. This creates a disconnect between authors and their readers, unless the book is designed to strategically drive engagement beyond its pages. This is where strategic calls to action (CTAs) come in.

CTAs serve as clear, compelling invitations for your readers to take the next step. If your book lacks them, it means you're missing opportunities to engage your audience beyond it. It also means you have no direct way to capture leads, attract speaking gigs, or sell additional services. Your book may still be valuable for your reader, but without CTAs it won't actively bring them into your ecosystem so you can serve them.

Well-crafted CTAs help convert passive readers into active participants in your world. Whether these participants move into your marketing funnel, sign up for a newsletter, or purchase additional services, these touchpoints allow you to build long-term relationships that can lead to speaking engagements, consulting opportunities, and more. The goal is to bring your readers into your ecosystem so that they continue to engage with you, your work, and your expertise.

Types of CTAs

There is no one-size-fits-all approach to CTAs, but they should align with your unique business or personal objectives as well as the next logical step for your reader. Here are some common types of CTAs you can integrate into your book or carry over into your marketing strategies if you're already published:

- **Encouraging Further Learning**
    - If you host a podcast (or have been a guest on relevant shows), directing readers to listen can help deepen their connection with you.
    - If you've appeared in some kind of video content, such as an interview or a webinar, and had an insightful discussion, linking to it can strengthen your credibility.
    - If you offer structured training, a free or paid workshop or online course can be a natural next step for your audience.

- **Providing Resources and Tools**
    - Offer readers practical tools that complement your book, such as downloadable guides, tools, templates, blueprints, or checklists.
    - Use engaging quizzes and assessments that allow readers to apply concepts from your book while you simultaneously capture their contact information for future engagement.
    - Offer exclusive content such as bonus chapters, expanded insights, or additional case studies on your website.

Well-crafted calls to action help convert passive readers into active participants in your world.

- **Strengthening Engagement**
  - Join or create a community or email list where you encourage readers to sign up for updates, exclusive content, or a private online group.
  - Encourage social media following by providing clear links to your platforms to continue the conversation beyond the book.
  - If your book ties into your business or thought leadership, ensure readers know how to hire you for professional services by including a CTA such as "Contact me for consulting or speaking engagements."
- **Incorporating Philanthropic Tie-Ins**
  - Consider cause-driven purchases by donating a percentage of book sales to a nonprofit aligned with your book's theme.
  - Use community initiatives to highlight any charitable projects you support, allowing readers to feel part of something bigger when they buy your book.
  - If your book ties into industry challenges (e.g., affordable housing, mental health awareness), partnering with an aligned organization through a corporate sponsorship can elevate both your message and impact.

Where to Place CTAs

CTAs can be positioned throughout your book in strategic locations to maximize engagement:

- **Inside the Manuscript**

  Seamlessly integrate links or references to free resources, tools, or next steps within relevant sections of your book.

- **Front Matter**

  Before the main text of your book begins, place a compelling CTA that readers can see before they even dive into the content.

- **Back Matter**

  After the main text of your book ends, ensure your final pages include strong CTAs directing readers to their next step. Here are some common back-matter CTAs:

  - Hire the author to speak
  - Book club discussion questions
  - Other books by the author
  - Promotions for online courses, coaching, or consulting services

To see examples of each, refer to appendix C.

What If Your Book Is Already Published Without CTAs?

If your book is already out in the world and you didn't include any CTAs, you're not out of options. While it may feel daunting to go back and make changes, your book is a living asset, one that can evolve alongside your business and goals.

Option 1: Republish with Intentionality

The most effective approach is to take the time to republish your book with strategic updates. Republishing allows you to update your book with intentionality by integrating meaningful CTAs throughout the text and adding new front and back matter. This ensures your book aligns with your broader marketing strategies.

Option 2: Create External CTAs

If republishing isn't feasible right away, you can still retrofit CTAs into your marketing strategies. Here are some of the most common ways to do this:

- Update your online retail listings pages (Amazon, Barnes & Noble, etc.) by adding a strong CTA in your book's description that makes it clear they can engage with you.

- Create a companion resource, such as a free guide, worksheet, or exclusive content, and promote it to your audience.
- Use social media and email marketing to engage your readers after they finish your book by directing them to sign up for updates or join a webinar.
- Leverage speaking engagements, especially if you use your book in your business, by mentioning ways your readers and audience can connect with you.
- Consider adding a custom sticker inside the book with a QR code or short URL that directs readers to your website, free resources, or upcoming events.

Even a small, well-placed CTA can create powerful momentum. You've likely noticed CTAs intentionally placed throughout this book, each one designed to guide you to engage more deeply. As you continue through this chapter, you'll explore additional strategies to deepen your impact, expand your reach, and turn your book into a lasting bridge between you and your audience.

Aligning Your Book with a Cause

Your book shouldn't just sit on a shelf. It should be an active part of your brand and marketing strategy, which you can accomplish through cause marketing. Cause marketing means tying your book to a meaningful social or philanthropic initiative, making it not just a product but a tool for impact. Aligning your book with a cause ensures it will continue to serve you and your audience in meaningful ways.

Cause-Marketing Benefits

Aligning your book with a cause makes marketing feel mission-driven rather than like a commercial endeavor. When readers see that your book is about more than just sales, they're more likely to engage, share, and support your work, amplifying its impact. Readers today, especially millennials and Gen Z-ers, are more likely to support brands and books that align with a cause they care about, In fact, studies show that over 80 percent of consumers will switch to a brand when they learn it supports a social cause they care about.[8] This means your book can be a bridge to making a real difference while deepening engagement with your audience.

Cause marketing also opens doors to speaking engagements, media opportunities, and meaningful collaborations with values-aligned organizations. By strategically partnering with organizations, companies, and individuals who share your vision, you can extend your book's reach, create mutually beneficial opportunities, and strengthen your credibility. During this Strategize phase of the ASPEN Method, cause alignment helps you choose the right partnerships, messages, and audiences, and during later phases it helps you continue to grow by deepening reader loyalty, expanding your network, and creating ripple effects for your mission. Whether your goal is to donate proceeds, cohost events, or simply shine a light on a shared value, cause marketing is one of the most sustainable ways to extend your book's reach and impact well beyond your launch.

If your book is already published and you haven't yet built in a cause-driven approach, it's not too late. You can republish with intentionality or create external CTAs.

Expanding the Impact: Specific Strategies for Cause-Driven Authors

Cause marketing isn't a one-size-fits-all strategy or a one-time tactic. It's a spectrum of possibilities and a long-term plan that integrates across the entire ASPEN Method. During a PYP training, Grace Lanni, my go-to expert on cause marketing, noted the vital role of being authentic in this alignment: "Cause marketing only works when it's authentic. Don't choose a cause because it sounds good—choose one that reflects who you really are." When your message and your mission truly reflect

---

8. Grocery Headquarters Staff, "Cone Cause Evolution Study: Consumers Want More Cause-Related Products," *Supermarket News*, January 1, 2018, https://www.supermarketnews.com/consumer-trends/cone-cause-evolution-study-consumers-want-more-cause-related-products?utm_source=chatgpt.com.

STRATEGIZE YOUR VISIBILITY AND AUDIENCE GROWTH

your values, your audience can feel the difference and will respond with greater trust and enthusiasm.

Here are actionable strategies to align your book with a cause in ways that feel authentic and effective, followed by real-world examples of PYP books in action:

- **Donations**

    A classic but powerful approach to cause marketing is inviting donations. Pledging 10 percent of your book sales to a nonprofit aligned with your message builds goodwill and invites your readers to join a shared mission.

    Several authors at PYP have pledged proceeds to causes that align with their messages, from donating a portion of profits to organizations supporting affordable housing for survivors of domestic violence to contributing all book sales to a cancer research fund in memory of a loved one.

- **In-Kind Giving**

    Instead of monetary gifts, consider tangible contributions tied to purchases, such as "One book sold = One meal donated" or "Every book sold funds school supplies for a child in need." These small gestures can create big emotional resonance with readers.

    One PYP author donates a can of pet food for every book sold to local animal shelters. As part of their healing mission, another gives free copies of their memoir to people in recovery programs.

- **Service-Based Campaigns**

    If your book draws from your professional background, whether legal, consulting, health, education, or any other, you can give back by offering pro bono hours speaking at events or mentoring people connected to your cause.

A workplace inclusion expert who published with PYP paired her book with pro bono DEI consulting hours for nonprofits. Another was a lawyer who created a model in which his book sales help subsidize legal services for those who've experienced abuse.

- **Education and Community Impact**

    Team up with nonprofits or advocacy groups to place your book in front of new audiences. These organizations often have newsletters, social platforms, and community events that offer perfect visibility opportunities for aligned books.

    An author at PYP with a book tied to the education system partnered with a school district to bring their story and custom curriculum into classrooms. Another launched a local campaign in which every book sold funded a meal for LGBTQ+ youth experiencing homelessness.

- **Pre-Order Campaigns**

    Pre-order campaigns are a powerful opportunity to merge your launch strategy with your values. By tying early sales to a specific cause, you can activate your community while amplifying your message.

    Some PYP authors linked their pre-orders to impact by pledging a donation to a local nonprofit for each early sale, turning a marketing strategy into a community movement.

These examples prove that cause marketing doesn't have to be complex, it just has to be sincere. When your book aligns with a cause, you invite your readers into a shared mission that can amplify your message and make a tangible difference. Small, intentional actions can make a significant impact, transforming your book into a catalyst for change.

To bring your ideas to life, it helps to break down your campaign into clear, strategic components. The following chart offers a simple framework to guide your thinking as you design a cause-driven campaign that feels personal, purposeful, and aligned with your book's message. Use it as a starting point to map out a plan that's both actionable and authentic.

CAUSE + ACTION = CAMPAIGN		
Your Cause	What do you care about?	Example: Literacy access, mental health, social justice
Campaign Action	What can you offer or do?	Example: Donate $1 per pre-order, host a co-branded event, share platform visibility
Strategic Fit	Why this cause?	Example: Mirrors my book's themes, connects with my core audience, aligns with my business goals
Campaign Name or Hook	Keep it short and catchy.	Examples: "Pages for Progress" "Read with Pride" "Books for Belonging"

Strategic Partnerships and Bulk Sales

Strategic partnerships and bulk sales can be game changers for authors looking to maximize both impact and revenue. By forming alliances with corporations, nonprofits, and industry organizations, you can leverage their networks to distribute your book on a much larger scale, transforming it into a tool for education, empowerment, and change. The most common buckets of bulk opportunities are within corporate and nonprofit spaces or via conferences and event collaborations.

Corporate and Nonprofit Partnerships

Bulk purchases can lead to substantial exposure and revenue. By partnering with corporations or nonprofits to purchase large quantities of your book, you can provide them with valuable resources while boosting your sales. A company focused on leadership development, for example, might purchase 1,000 copies of a book on effective management to distribute to its employees, enhancing both their skills and your visibility.

Conference and Event Collaborations

When speaking at industry events or conferences, work with organizers to include your book as part of the registration package. Rather than relying on individual sales at the event, using this strategy guarantees a higher volume of books will end up in attendees' hands. This enhances your influence, solidifies your expertise, provides immediate revenue, and sparks post-event discussions centered around your content. Similarly, if you're scheduled to speak at an industry event, collaborating with organizers to purchase copies of your book for attendees positions you as a thought leader while providing valuable resources. For example, at a leadership summit, a book on management practices could be distributed to hundreds of attendees, ensuring the author's insights are shared widely and immediately.

Cause-Driven Bulk Sales

Bulk book purchases provide an opportunity for large-scale impact and additional revenue. Take inspiration from TOMS Shoes' "Buy one, give one" model by incorporating a cause-driven element into your bulk sales strategy: For every 500 books purchased by an organization, you can donate an equivalent number to a nonprofit, school, or library serving an underserved audience. This not only expands your book's reach but aligns with corporate partners looking to demonstrate social impact.

For authors whose books are aligned with social causes, these partnerships can also take the form of joint fundraisers, co-branded events, or bundled donations, such as "Buy one, donate one" campaigns. These strategies increase visibility and deepen emotional connection with your audience and collaborators.

Keep in mind that strategic partnerships aren't just about selling books; they're about creating lasting relationships that amplify your book's message and impact. Approach these partnerships as mutually beneficial opportunities to further both your goals and those of your partners. By thinking big and acting boldly, you can transform your book from a single sale into a movement, one that reaches more readers, builds lasting partnerships, and creates measurable impact.

Working with Bookstores

Building strong, reciprocal relationships with independent bookstores requires more than just dropping off a copy of your book and hoping for shelf space. Booksellers are often operating with limited staff and tight margins, and many stores, especially those with a values-based mission, receive frequent pitches from authors.

If you want your book to stand out, you need to approach the relationship as a collaboration, not a transaction. That starts with doing your homework to understand the bookstore's values, audience, and submission process. Many stores have formal intake forms or FAQs on their websites, which may ask about your book's themes, target audience, marketing plans, and even your stance on social issues. These questions aren't about gatekeeping—they're about alignment. A mission-driven bookstore wants to know that your book is a fit for their community and that you, as the author, are invested in supporting their space in return. During a PYP presentation called "Working with Bookstores," Emily Autenrieth, owner of A Seat at the Table Books in Sacramento, CA, said, "We're not just looking for books—we're building community. When an author shows up with alignment, professionalism, and a genuine desire to partner, we notice. That's what transforms a pitch into a relationship."

Book Launch and Pre-Order Strategies

A well-strategized book launch can set the foundation for long-term success, and pre-orders play a crucial role in building momentum before your official release date. However, even if your book is already published, you still have opportunities to increase sales and strengthen your connection with readers by selling directly from your website.

For authors who have yet to publish, pre-orders can generate buzz and excitement that helps drive early sales and establish credibility. A strong pre-order campaign can also boost your ranking on bestseller lists upon launch, as all pre-order sales count toward your first-week numbers.

> By thinking big and acting boldly, you can transform your book from a single sale into a movement, one that reaches more readers, builds lasting partnerships, and creates measurable impact.

Driving Direct Sales

For those whose books are already available, focusing on direct sales through your website allows you to retain more revenue per sale. It also allows you to collect valuable customer information and build lasting relationships with readers, two things third-party retailers such as Amazon and bookstores don't provide. Instead of simply directing readers to an external retailer, offering exclusive bonuses or signed copies through your website makes purchasing directly from you more appealing.

Regardless of where you are on your publishing journey, consider these strategies to drive direct book sales:

- **Special Edition Releases**

    Offer a hardcover, color edition, or signed copies exclusively through your website. This makes the purchase feel more special than a standard retail buy.

- **Format Staggering**

    If your book is newly released, you can strategically stagger different formats, such as paperback, ebook, and audiobook, to extend visibility and keep promotional opportunities fresh.

- **Launch or Relaunch Events**

    Whether your book is new or has been out for a while, hosting a virtual or in-person event can create buzz and reinvigorate interest. Use this opportunity to read excerpts, share insights, and engage with your audience in a way that deepens their connection to your book.

- **Exclusive Content and Bonuses**

    - Make your website the preferred place to buy your book by offering special perks such as these:
    - A sticker and/or bookmark bundle available only via the website
    - A bonus chapter or downloadable guide
    - A signed bookplate or personalized note

- Access to an exclusive webinar or Q&A session
- A limited-time discount or bundled offer with other products or services

Building Connections Through Virtual Events

Whether your launch is in-person, hybrid, or entirely virtual, how you engage your audience matters just as much as what you share. For online launches in particular, adding a layer of interactivity can transform your event from a passive webinar into a dynamic, relationship-building moment.

Zoom breakout rooms are one underused but powerful tactic for this. You can pre-assign attendees to small groups based on interest or audience type (e.g., readers, clients, friends, or professional peers) and use a simple icebreaker or prompt to kick off the event. This encourages authentic connection and warms up the energy before you even begin speaking.

Another powerful approach is to invite people featured in your book to cohost or participate. For memoirs this might include close friends, mentors, or key figures in your story, and for thought leadership books you could spotlight a contributor, testimonial giver, or early supporter. Featuring these voices adds credibility, broadens the conversation, and takes pressure off you as the sole speaker. You might also consider appointing a designated event host to guide the flow. A trusted friend or colleague can manage transitions, read introductions, monitor chat questions, and help keep the energy upbeat. This frees you up to focus on storytelling, gratitude, and connection rather than logistics.

Here are some other online launch engagement ideas that have proven successful:

- Breakout rooms where attendees can connect before or after the reading
- Live readings or excerpts shared by you or a featured guest
- Panel-style Q&A sessions in which you and any contributors discuss key themes

- Virtual giveaways or trivia tied to your book's topic
- Spotlights on community members who helped bring the book to life

Your book launch is more than an announcement. It's an opportunity to build a deeper community around your message. Interactive elements foster belonging, spark word of mouth, and allow your readers to feel like they're part of something bigger.

Choosing the Right Excerpt

You might choose to read a short excerpt during your launch event, but don't feel obligated to default to the first chapter. Often the most emotionally resonant or curiosity-sparking passages come from the middle of your book. Use early reader or beta reader feedback to guide your selection. What passages made people tear up? Laugh out loud? Text you right after reading? Choose something that evokes a reaction and gives your audience a reason to want more. A compelling read-aloud moment isn't just about content but also about connection. When people feel something during your event, they're more likely to remember it, talk about it, and share your book with others.

Strategy Is About Long-Term Impact

Marketing your book is about more than generating immediate sales. It's about ensuring your message has staying power. As Erica Holthausen, founder of Catchline Communications, explained during a PYP internal training session, "Publishing is not just about getting exposure. It's about establishing your authority and building relationships with your readers before they ever pick up your book." From pre-orders and partnerships to bulk sales and cause marketing, each step should align with your larger goals as an author and thought leader. Rather than scrambling for visibility post-launch, start with a clear vision: Is your book designed to grow your business, build credibility, or create social change? Defining your goals helps you focus on sustainable actions that deliver lasting results.

PROMOTE YOUR PURPOSE

If your time is limited, that's okay, start small. Focus on one high-impact activity each week, such as sending a podcast pitch, reaching out to a potential partner, or updating your call to action. Slow, focused progress is more effective—and more sustainable—than trying to do everything at once. Choose one call to action, one cause, or one partnership idea that excites you, and take a single step toward bringing it to life this week.

The most effective marketing is the kind that feels like an extension of who you are.

PROMOTE YOUR PURPOSE

By now you've explored several powerful ways to increase visibility, grow your audience, and connect your book to your broader goals. Let's distill those insights into a set of concrete, strategic choices that form the next section of your Strategic Book Marketing Plan. Use the space provided to begin sketching out your strategy, copy these prompts into your notebook, or use the online workbook to continue to build on what you started.

My CTAs

Identify two to three CTAs that are aligned with your book's purpose and your long-term business or impact goals. Include where they will appear (e.g., in the book, on your website, in your social posts) and what they invite readers to do.

....

....

....

....

....

....

....

STRATEGIZE YOUR VISIBILITY AND AUDIENCE GROWTH

What are the most logical next steps for your readers?

- ☐ Subscribe to your email list
- ☐ Download a resource
- ☐ Book a speaking engagement
- ☐ Join your community or program
- ☐ Other: ....

Where will you place your CTAs?

- ☐ Inside the manuscript
- ☐ Front matter
- ☐ Back matter
- ☐ Online marketing content
- ☐ Other: ....

Draft at least one call to action here:

Example: "Want to go deeper? Download the free companion guide at [yourwebsite.com/bonus]."

....
....
....
....
....
....
....
....

Is My Book a Good Fit for Cause Marketing?

The most effective marketing is the kind that feels like an extension of who you are. You don't need to follow a rigid formula. Lean into the strategies that align with your strengths and values. If speaking lights you up, prioritize event-based outreach. If writing is your comfort zone, focus on blog posts or articles that tie back to your book's message. To determine whether cause marketing is right for you and your book, answer these questions and take notes.

QUESTION	YES	NO	NOTES
Does your book align with a social issue, community need, or movement?			
Do you already support or belong to an organization aligned with your message?			
Would your audience feel more connected if your launch supported a cause?			
Could you partner with a nonprofit, local organization, or mission-driven brand?			
Is there a natural tie-in between your book's topic and a community initiative?			

If you answered yes to three or more of these questions, cause marketing could meaningfully enhance your launch and visibility. Be sure to choose approaches that feel natural to you so that you maintain your momentum without burning out. Use this space provided to capture your ideas:

STRATEGIZE YOUR VISIBILITY AND AUDIENCE GROWTH

My Cause:

....
....
....
....

Campaign Action:

....
....
....
....

Strategic Fit:

....
....
....
....

Campaign Name or Hook:

....
....
....
....

Stay intentional and rooted in your bigger purpose, and your book will continue to serve as a powerful tool for impact.

My Strategic Partnerships

List two to three potential partners who align with your book's message, mission, or audience. These could be nonprofits, professional organizations, educational institutions, companies, or community groups. Here's an example to help get you started:

- **Potential Partner:** Yale School of Management
- **Why It's a Good Fit:** My book includes real-world leadership case studies that could enhance MBA coursework or guest lectures.
- **Next Step:** Connect with a faculty member teaching at the business school and offer to guest lecture or provide a bulk discount for student use.

Potential Partner	Why It's a Good Fit	Next Step

Once you've identified your top partners and outlined your next steps, consider what type of collaboration would be the most mutually beneficial. Use the following checklist to explore potential partnership models that align with your goals and the partner's mission:

- ☐ Bulk book purchase
- ☐ Co-branded event, training, or webinar
- ☐ Newsletter or blog feature
- ☐ Book club or classroom adoption
- ☐ Joint giveaway or campaign

- [ ] Sponsored speaking engagement or panel appearance
- [ ] Resource bundle or curriculum integration
- [ ] Affiliate or referral partnership

My Strategies for Book Launch and Bulk Sales

Now that you've explored how to partner with aligned organizations, it's time to turn your attention to how you'll share your book with a wider audience. Whether your book is about to launch or has been out for a while, strategic sales tactics—especially through direct and bulk channels—can help you build momentum, boost visibility, and generate sustainable revenue.

Use this section to brainstorm how you'll either launch your book or reinvigorate its momentum through bulk sales, events, and special promotions.

- **My current publishing status:**
  - [ ] Pre-launch
  - [ ] Recently launched
  - [ ] Already published

- **Direct sales opportunities:**
  - [ ] Special edition (signed, color, hardcover)
  - [ ] Exclusive website bonus (download, video, chapter)
  - [ ] Webinar, Q&A, or launch party
  - [ ] Podcast, newsletter, or blog announcement

- **Bulk sales targets:**
  - [ ] Conference / Event inclusion
  - [ ] Corporate / Nonprofit training
  - [ ] School / Library purchase
  - [ ] "Buy one, donate one" campaign

▸ **What's one immediate step you can take?**

Example: "Reach out to [organization] about a bulk purchase tied to their employee training program."

....

....

....

Remember: Success isn't just measured in book sales. A successful book marketing plan includes how your book elevates your mission, grows your influence, and opens new doors. It might lead to consulting opportunities, build an engaged community, or spark strategic partnerships. By thinking beyond the initial launch, you'll unlock your book's potential as a long-term asset.

Marketing is an ongoing process, not a one-time campaign. Whether your book is brand new or has been out for a while, it's never too late to refine your approach. Stay intentional and rooted in your bigger purpose, and your book will continue to serve as a powerful tool for impact.

PUT PURPOSE INTO PRACTICE

Now that you've mapped out your strategic next steps, take a moment to zoom out. Which opportunities feel most aligned with the goals you've set? Where can you make the biggest impact with the least friction? Identify one strategic move you'll act on this week to build sustainable momentum.

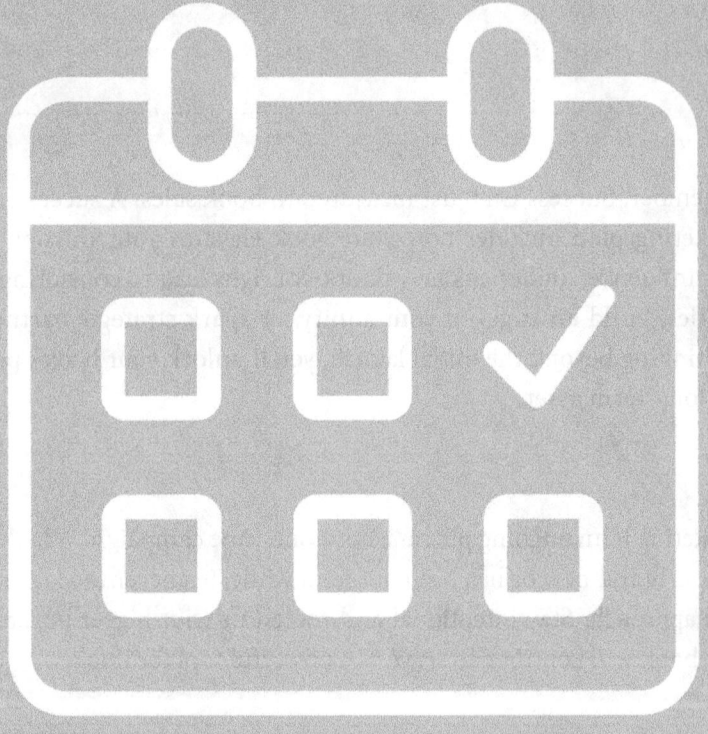

PLAN

CHAPTER 10: Plan and Promote Your Book with Intention

PICK YOUR PATH

If your marketing strategy is already mapped out, skip to chapter 11 to start executing.

Now that you have clarity on your strategy for the CTAs you're weaving into your book, the causes you're aligned with, and the partnerships you're targeting, it's time to put those ideas into motion. The Strategize phase is where you laid the groundwork for your book's success. Now, in the Planning phase of the ASPEN Method, we'll turn those insights into a structured roadmap, ensuring your marketing efforts are purposeful, coordinated, and positioned for long-term impact.

Effective book marketing isn't about throwing ideas at the wall and hoping something sticks. It's about intentionality. Planning is where ideas become real. It's where you define who will buy your book, who can help amplify its reach, and how to organize your efforts so momentum builds naturally rather than feeling forced. You'll also create a strategy to engage key audiences, secure book reviews, and build relationships that extend your book's visibility long after the initial launch.

In this chapter, we will explore the following elements of planning:

> **Creating Your Book Buyer List and Network**
>
> Learn how to identify your most reliable supporters, those who are not only likely to buy your book but are willing to help spread the word. You'll discover how to build and organize a

buyer list that makes outreach more efficient and increases your chances of success.

- **Connecting with Your Influencers as Amplifiers**

  Explore how to identify the people and platforms who already have the trust of your ideal readers, such as podcast hosts, community leaders, educators, or aligned organizations, and how to build meaningful relationships that extend your reach and credibility.

- **Maximizing Book Reviews**

  Understand how to ask for reviews in a way that feels natural and aligned, how to provide helpful prompts to guide readers, and why reviews play a vital role in visibility, social proof, and long-term book sales, no matter where people buy your book.

- **Designing Your Pre-Order or Crowdfunding Campaign**

  Discover how to structure a pre-order offer or crowdfunding campaign that generates early momentum, builds trust, and turns supporters into champions. You'll learn how to offer meaningful bonuses, price your packages, and fulfill orders in a way that works for your energy and goals.

- **Structuring Your Book Marketing Roadmap**

  Learn how to promote intentionally by tailoring your timeline, capacity, and goals. This includes building systems for outreach, setting clear priorities, fulfilling promises, and using checklists and trackers to stay organized and on task, without burning out.

- **Maintaining Long-Term Visibility**

  Develop a sustainable approach to book marketing that continues well beyond your launch. From setting marketing rhythms and boundaries to designing recovery rituals and tracking return on effort, you'll learn how to keep your book visible in ways that feel manageable and aligned with your purpose.

This phase is about developing intentional strategies that connect your book to larger opportunities, revenue streams, and long-term engagement rather than relying on scattered efforts. As you move through this chapter, you'll explore key tactics that, when combined with the other phases of the ASPEN Method, will form a cohesive, step-by-step roadmap tailored to your goals.

Now, let's map your next moves with purpose.

Your Book Buyer List and Network

In chapter 6, we talked about identifying your reader and buyer, and I asked you to determine who's likely to buy your book and why. That's because in this Planning phase, success starts with knowing who will buy it. Many authors assume their book will naturally find an audience, but strategic planning is key to maximizing sales and engagement. By identifying and organizing your potential buyers in advance, you can ensure a smoother launch, avoid last-minute scrambling, and leverage your network effectively.

Where to Find Your Book Buyers

Your buyers typically fall into three main categories:

1. Your personal network, which includes friends, family, colleagues, and longtime supporters who want to see you succeed

2. People who are already interested in your topic, such as clients, students, members of niche communities, or individuals actively following discussions in your subject area

3. Engaged readers from your existing content, including blog subscribers, newsletter readers, social media followers, or podcast listeners who already consume and trust your content

One of our authors built her initial buyer list by pulling her LinkedIn contacts, old conference rosters, and alumni network into one spreadsheet. By identifying just 15 people who were active in niche HR spaces, she sparked early momentum, securing 60 pre-orders before her official launch. To do

To make this easier, download our buyer spreadsheet template at **promoteyourpurposebook.com/bonuses** to help you organize your contacts, track outreach, and turn relationships into book sales.

something similar and stay organized, you can compile all your email contacts, LinkedIn connections, and social media followers into one primary spreadsheet. This will serve as your buyer list, making it easy to track engagement and outreach. You can separate your list into different tabs based on categories of buyers or add a column to identify them at a quick glance.

How Book Buyers Support You Beyond Buying

Your buyers can do more than just purchase a copy of your book. Many of them may be willing to support your launch and marketing strategies in additional ways:

- They can introduce you to relevant groups or communities. If they're part of a professional association, mastermind group, or online forum, they may be able to connect you with a broader audience.
- They may run a book club or be part of a professional reading group or online book community in which your book would be a great fit. Many people participate in these spaces, and your buyers can connect you with them.
- They can share your book with their personal or professional networks. They might be willing to post about your book on social media or forward an email about your launch.
- They may also be your reader. If you're building a business from your book, your buyers might be able to serve in both roles.

By approaching your buyers with clear but low-pressure requests, you increase the likelihood of their engagement without making them feel obligated. A well-planned buyer outreach strategy ensures consistent communication, builds anticipation for your book, and turns early readers into enthusiastic advocates.

> Effective book marketing isn't about throwing ideas at the wall and hoping something sticks. It's about intentionality.

Your Influencers and Their Role

Once you've identified your book buyers, the next step is determining who can help amplify your reach. These individuals, whether industry experts, media figures, podcast hosts, or local community leaders, have trusted audiences that can introduce your book to a wider market.

What Is an Influencer in Book Marketing?

The term *influencer* often conjures images of social media personalities with large followings, but in book marketing it's much broader. Influencers include the following:

- Podcast hosts who interview experts in your field
- Conference organizers who curate speaker lineups
- Educators who assign books in their courses
- Newsletter writers with dedicated subscriber bases
- Peer authors who cross-promote to aligned audiences
- Community leaders who introduce your work to niche groups

These individuals and organizations already speak to the audience you want to reach. They hold influence not because of how many followers they have, but because of the trust they've earned in their circles.

How Influencers Can Support You Beyond Social Media

Like book buyers, influencers can support your book in multiple ways, and often outside of traditional marketing channels:

- **Feature You on a Podcast, Webinar, or Live Event**

    A 30-minute interview or author spotlight can introduce your work to a new, targeted audience.

- **Include Your Book in a Newsletter or Blog**

    Many thought leaders share curated book lists or author interviews in their content.

- **Invite You to Speak or Guest Teach**

  Your book can be a tool for continuing education programs, conference workshops, or university guest lectures.

- **Recommend Your Book to Their Professional Network**

  An email introduction or shout-out in a Slack group, mastermind, or industry circle can lead to meaningful visibility.

- **Collaborate on Events or Joint Campaigns**

  Whether it's a virtual panel or a book giveaway, cohosted efforts often lead to deeper engagement.

As with book buyers, the key is to approach influencers with respect and alignment. Don't just ask for promotion, offer value. Think of it as a relationship, not a transaction.

Remember: Your influencers aren't just promotional tools. They're potential partners in amplifying your message and impact. Build these relationships with care and intention, and they'll become powerful allies on your publishing journey.

Don't Assume—Invite Instead

Your buyers and influencers are the foundation of your book's success. Buyers help by purchasing, reviewing, and recommending your book, while influencers help by expanding your reach through their trusted audiences. By strategically organizing your outreach to make it easy for people to support you, and by engaging them authentically, you'll maximize visibility and ensure long-term momentum.

One of the biggest mistakes authors make is assuming who will (or won't) support their book. I've seen authors skip over people in their network because they "didn't want to bother them" or assumed that person wasn't interested. It's easy to believe people won't care, can't help, or are too busy. But assumptions limit your reach before you've even tried.

The key is to phrase your ask as a gentle, open-ended, and meaningful invitation. Rather than pressuring them, use a form, waitlist, or personal message to invite people into your ecosystem, then let them self-select instead of deciding for them. Whether it's asking, "Would you be open to sharing this?" or "Is there a group that might benefit from this message?" your goal is to create space for people to say yes. You're not imposing, you're inviting them into a mission they might be thrilled to support.

Success with book marketing isn't just about a strong launch; it's about sustained engagement. Building genuine relationships with your supporters will turn them into long-term advocates. You'll be surprised by who shows up when you create space for them to do so.

Requesting and Leveraging Book Reviews

Once you've identified your supporters, the next step is encouraging them to leave reviews. Book reviews play a critical role in establishing your credibility, boosting your ranking on Amazon and helping new readers discover your work. A book with strong reviews also has a higher chance of being recommended by algorithms that increase sales organically.

Even if you prefer readers to purchase your book from independent bookstores, your website, or other retailers, having reviews on Amazon is still essential. Many potential buyers use those platforms as research tools before making a purchase elsewhere. A book with numerous reviews makes it easier for readers to trust your book's value no matter where they choose to buy it.

Working Through the Discomfort of Reviews

As you might have already experienced, publishing a book is a vulnerable act. You're putting your voice, ideas, and story into the world, and inevitably that means people will respond. Some reviews will light you up, and others might sting. And sometimes, the most biting feedback comes from someone who missed the point entirely.

This is part of the process.

It's not just the reviews that make this hard, it's what they represent: visibility. And visibility often carries its own quiet weight. For many of us, the hardest part of sharing our work isn't what we say but what it feels like to be seen. We brace for judgment, we overthink how we'll be perceived, and we fear we'll be told we're not ready, not credible, not enough. Even when we know what we want to say, there can be a deeper hesitation underneath it all. This isn't just fear of bad reviews; it's the internal resistance that comes with emotional exposure. I've experienced it firsthand, not in front of a crowd but behind a keyboard. I had to learn that visibility isn't about being fearless. It's about being courageous enough to show up anyway.

Whether you're receiving glowing praise or a one-star review from someone who clearly didn't read past the first chapter, it's easy to get pulled into emotional highs and lows. But here's the truth: A single review, good or bad, does not define the value of your work. Your book is not for everyone.

When reading reviews, it helps to keep these points in mind:

- Pay attention to patterns, not outliers. If one person didn't like your tone but twenty others said your voice felt authentic and powerful, believe the twenty.

- Ground yourself in your purpose. Go back to why you wrote the book in the first place. Was it to make a specific group feel seen? To open a conversation that needed to be started? That purpose still stands, regardless of someone else's opinion.

- Celebrate the courageous act of finishing and publishing. Many people dream of writing a book, but far fewer follow through. You did. That's worth honoring.

- Don't assign equal weight to every voice. Not all feedback deserves your energy, and not every reviewer is your reader. Give yourself permission to release what doesn't serve you.

It's okay to feel discomfort. Let it pass through you, but don't let it define your relationship with your work. Instead, collect what affirms your purpose—highlighted reviews, thank-you messages from readers, photos of your book on someone's desk—and keep them in a folder you can return to on tough days.

This is about building emotional resilience, not about perfection. Every review is a reminder that your work is out in the world doing something. Keep going.

> For many of us, the hardest part of sharing our work isn't what we say but what it feels like to be seen.

Who to Ask for Reviews:

- Friends and colleagues who can provide thoughtful, honest reviews
- Early readers who were engaged in your writing process (e.g., beta readers, editors, writing group members)
- Newsletter subscribers or social media followers who've already shown interest in your book

How to Make It Easy for Them:

- Provide clear instructions on where to leave a review (e.g., Amazon, Goodreads, your website).
- Offer review prompts to guide them, such as "What was the most valuable takeaway from this book?" or "Who would benefit the most from reading this book?"
- Send follow-up reminders, but avoid offering incentives (Amazon has strict policies against incentivized reviews).

A simple, well-planned request for reviews ensures your book will build momentum immediately after launch by encouraging new readers to engage with your work. Focus your review outreach on readers who will find value in your message and are well-positioned to share it. Otherwise, your review strategy won't help create a pipeline, a steady stream of interest that leads readers to your services, programs, or speaking opportunities. As Robbie Samuels, an award-winning and four-time bestselling author and book launch strategist, put it during one of PYP's internal trainings, "If your reviews aren't tied to a larger strategy, you're missing the chance to turn visibility into opportunity."

Planning Your Pre-Order or Crowdfunding Campaign

Now that you have a plan for who you'll reach out to and how, let's talk about how to apply that to planning and structuring your pre-order or crowdfunding campaign to create energy, excitement, and engagement.

Pre-orders aren't just about early sales. They're a way to build trust and momentum before launch day or a promotional endeavor. Oriana Leckert, head of publishing at Kickstarter, put it like this during a PYP training: "People don't just want a product—they want a story to be part of. Pre-orders are your chance to invite them into something bigger than a transaction." You can offer pre-orders directly through your website or via a crowdfunding platform such as Kickstarter.

Your Pre-Order Path: Direct vs. Platform-Based

You can structure pre-orders in many ways, but the two most common are direct pre-orders on your website and crowdfunding platforms. The first gives you total control, better data, and alignment with your brand, and the second has built-in tools for tiered rewards, discovery, and urgency. The right path depends on your goals. What matters most is that your offer is clear, aligned with your values, and easy for readers to act on.

> Curious how real authors are creating successful pre-order campaigns? Watch our expert session with Oriana Leckert at **promoteyourpurposebook.com/bonuses**.

The Power of Book Bonuses

Offering bonuses during your pre-order window or crowdfunding campaign is one of the most effective ways to generate early marketing momentum and deepen your connection with readers. Crowdfunding allows you to raise funds upfront by inviting your community to support your book before it's published. In return, supporters receive rewards, such as signed books, exclusive content, or behind-the-scenes access, that align with their level of contribution. Bonuses not only incentivize people to buy your book but also position your book as part of something bigger. Whether it's exclusive content, early access, or unique experiences, bonus offers create a sense of intimacy and alignment between you and your audience.

Book bonuses can include any of the following:

- ▸ A downloadable workbook or companion resource
- ▸ A private Q&A or behind-the-scenes session with you

- Access to a mini-course or training tied to the book's topic
- Shout-outs or acknowledgments in the book (for crowdfunding supporters)
- Signed bookplates or personalized messages
- A bundle that includes your book plus additional services or products

Bonuses work because they turn a transaction into a relationship. Instead of just buying a book, supporters feel like they're participating in your journey, and that's a powerful shift.

Pre-Order Packages

Offering bonuses during your pre-order window, whether through your own website or a platform such as Kickstarter, is a powerful way to build early momentum, engage your readers more deeply, and potentially offset publishing costs.

If your book aligns with a cause, consider incorporating a donation element or nonprofit partnership into your pre-order bonus strategy. These efforts can turn your campaign into a movement, not just a marketing tool. For example, you might donate a portion of each pre-order to a nonprofit aligned with your message, or maybe you'll partner with an organization to cohost an early-access event for supporters. Readers who care about your cause will be even more excited to champion your book.

There are many crowdfunding platforms available, each with its own strengths, but I'm partial to Kickstarter. In addition to its strong publishing category and built-in discovery features, Kickstarter is a public benefit corporation, which means it considers social impact alongside profit as part of their business model. For values-driven authors, this model can feel like a natural extension of their book's purpose.

Pre-orders aren't just a sales tool. They're a trust-building mechanism. When someone pre-orders your book, they're saying, "I believe in this message enough to support it before it exists." Your job is to honor that belief with something that feels exciting, thoughtful, and worth the wait.

Purpose-Driven Options

You don't need a massive audience to make a pre-order or crowdfunding campaign successful. You just need the *right* offer, one that's aligned with your readers, your budget, and your comfort level. With the intent of helping you build meaningful relationships and offer a taste of your expertise, which is especially valuable for authors who are also coaches, consultants, or facilitators, here are common tiers that have worked well for purpose-driven authors like you:

1. **Low-Tier Offers (Simple + Profitable)**
   - A signed copy of the book
   - A bookmark or sticker tucked inside (be sure it's lightweight and eligible for Media Mail in the US)

Baseline Example: Most authors in our community begin with a low-tier offer that includes a signed copy of the book and a small bonus item, such as a sticker or a bookmark. This tier is designed to be easy to fulfill, cost-effective to ship, and appealing to early supporters who want something personal without a large commitment.

2. **Mid-Tier Offers (Engagement + Community):**
   - A live group Q&A with the author
   - A monthly book club or "Ask Me Anything" session
   - A mini consultation, such as a 15-minute call
   - A private podcast episode, audio chapter, or digital resource

Real Examples: Midge Noble,[9] author of *Gay with God*, hosted monthly Zoom chats in the months leading up to her launch. These became a mix of spiritual coaching, support, and deep connection with readers.

---

9. https://publishyourpurpose.com/authors/midge-noble/.

Julie Wanzer,[10] author of *Get Them to Care*, offered a $149 pre-order tier that included a personalized LinkedIn audit, connecting directly to her book's topic and value proposition.

3. High-Tier Offers (VIP Access + Volume):

- Buy 10 or more books → get invited to a private virtual event.
- Buy 25 books → get a behind-the-scenes author session or 1:1 coaching.
- Gift a copy to someone else and unlock a bonus (great for team or group gifts).
- Include exclusive physical items, such as branded scarves, bookmarks, or custom art.

Real Example: Prince Manvendra and Prince DeAndre, authors of *A Royal Commitment*,[11] created a premium package that included a signed hardcover featuring their family's royal seal and a handwoven scarf. It wasn't just a reward; it was a story artifact that deepened their book's legacy.

Regardless of which tier you use, if you're planning to offer pre-order bonuses or run a crowdfunding campaign, make sure to do three things:

1. Communicate clearly what each bonus includes.
2. Set deadlines to create urgency.
3. Make fulfillment manageable (especially if you're shipping physical items).

---

10. https://publishyourpurpose.com/authors/julie-wanzer-leed-ap/.
11. https://publishyourpurpose.com/books/a-royal-commitment-ten-years-of-marriage-and-activism/.

> Promotion doesn't mean shouting the loudest or being everywhere at once. It means showing up with purpose, clarity, and a plan that reflects the value of your work.

Promoting Intentionally

Promotion doesn't mean shouting the loudest or being everywhere at once. It means showing up with purpose, clarity, and a plan that reflects the value of your work. Thoughtful promotion is about creating connection, not just visibility. Whether you're managing pre-orders, launching through crowdfunding, or simply selling direct, there are some strategies that will help you promote in a way that feels both strategic and sustainable.

Bonuses as Strategic Touchpoints

Bookmarks or stickers aren't just good add-ons. They can also be used strategically before or after your launch. Some authors create a simple system of having readers who send proof of purchase (or fill out a form on their website) receive a small thank you in the mail. This creates a second touchpoint with your audience and gives you an opportunity to gather email addresses, testimonials, or user-generated content in a fun and generous way. Plus you avoid the hassle of full print order fulfillment while still offering a meaningful, personal bonus. Did you catch what I did at the beginning of this book? That sticker offer is a perfect example of how this can look.

Pricing and Buyer Resistance

For a book that retails for $20, many authors successfully price a signed pre-order bundle at $40–$50. This covers printing, packaging, and any included bonuses. If that feels like too much, choose a price that covers your costs and feels comfortable to you. Remember: You're not just selling a book; you're building a business. Plan to price accordingly. While it may feel tempting to set a low price point to attract more readers, keep in mind that pricing influences perception. Books priced too low, such as $11.95, can unintentionally signal lower quality or value, even if the content is exceptional. A price like $18.95 or $21.95 often strikes a better balance between affordability and credibility. And given today's inflation, many authors are undercharging. The cost of goods, shipping, and production has risen across the board, yet book retail pricing has remained relatively stagnant due to buyer resistance. That means as an author you must be especially thoughtful that underpricing can undermine your authority and erode your margins. Consider what your ideal reader expects to pay for a quality book and set a price that reflects the expertise, time, and investment you've put into it.

Ship Experiences, Not Just Products

Plan ahead for whether to offer free shipping. Thanks to Amazon Prime culture, the phrase "free shipping" increases conversion, but you can always build the cost into your price and frame it that way (e.g., "$49 with free shipping"). If you're fulfilling pre-orders yourself, a few logistic tricks can save you both time and money. Readers in the US can use USPS Media Mail for the most affordable domestic shipping rates, just ensure you follow their guidelines (books only, no bonus merchandise such as bookmarks or stickers in the same package). To avoid damage during transit, fold oversized mailers slightly or reinforce them with cardboard inserts to protect corners and spines. These small adjustments can reduce returns and elevate your reader's unboxing experience.

Fulfillment and Promises

Another element to plan for is whether you want to ship the books yourself or use a fulfillment service. Some authors love the hands-on experience of signing each copy, adding handwritten notes, and packaging with care. But if you expect a larger volume of pre-orders or want to conserve your time and energy, outsourcing may be a better fit. There's no "right way" to do it. The key is to choose the fulfillment method that matches your goals, bandwidth, and how you want the reader experience to feel. A personalized touch is great, until it becomes a logistics headache. Plan ahead so you can follow through on the promises you make to your supporters.

Sustainable Marketing Approaches

Book marketing is a marathon that unfolds over months or even years, not just a sprint around your launch. To stay engaged without burning out, you need a book marketing plan that honors both your goals and your capacity. That means letting go of "shoulds," tuning into what's actually working, and building momentum through consistency—not hustle. Whether you're pre-launch or months past your release date, these sustainable tactics are here to support your long game by helping you focus your energy, build lasting connections, and keep showing up in ways that feel doable, meaningful, and aligned with your purpose.

Pick Three to Propel You Forward

With so many tactics available, it's tempting to try everything at once or get stuck doing nothing because you're not sure where to begin. But focus creates momentum. Instead of scattering your energy, concentrate on the three actions most likely to move your book forward right now. Start by asking yourself these questions:

- Which tactics align most directly with my goals?
- Where do I already have traction or relationships to build on?
- What fits best with my current time, energy, and capacity?

Choose just three high-impact actions to prioritize over the next 30–60 days. Write them down, commit to them, and revisit them weekly. Here are some examples for inspiration:

- Reach out to five podcast hosts.
- Host a soft-launch webinar or partner event.
- Send a personal pre-order invitation to 25 key contacts.
- Pitch myself for a local bookstore or community event.
- Launch a download or opt-in tied to my book's theme.

Don't worry about doing everything. Do what matters most, and do it with intention. These small, consistent choices are what build momentum over time.

Respect the Timeline—Make It Worth It

The earlier someone supports you, the more special their experience should be. That doesn't mean you need to offer massive bonuses, but you should make the exchange meaningful. If you're running a campaign with reward tiers (such as a crowdfunding platform), make sure to:

- Communicate clearly what each bonus includes.
- Set deadlines to create urgency.
- Make fulfillment manageable (especially for physical items).

Even small touches such as a private thank-you video, a bonus chapter, or a mention in your acknowledgments can go a long way.

Pace Yourself: Fulfillment Before Festivities

If you're managing health concerns, caregiving responsibilities, or simply feeling the emotional weight of your book launch and marketing path, consider separating the pre-order fulfillment phase from your celebration. Sending out early copies is a huge lift both logistically and energetically. You don't need to rush into hosting a launch event the same week. For one of our authors, honoring her body's need for rest during cancer treatment meant fulfilling her pre-orders first, then planning a celebration months later when she could be fully present. Your launch doesn't have to be a single day. It can unfold across time in a way that feels supportive and sustainable.

Make It Easy to Say Yes and Easy to Share

Some of your biggest champions may not buy dozens of books, but they might tell dozens of people about you. Equip them to do that:

- Offer "swipe copy" they can copy/paste to share on social media.
- Ask open-ended questions like, "Is there a group who would love this message?"
- Create low-pressure opt-ins such as interest forms or pre-order waitlists.

Memoirists and personal growth authors can also offer low-barrier, high-value opt-ins that build connection without requiring a major time investment. For example, downloadable affirmations, a short email series, curated journal prompts, or favorite quotes from the book can serve as engaging and accessible content. These simple offers help grow your list while extending the emotional experience of your book.

Evaluate What's Worth Continuing

Especially after launch, one of the smartest things you can do is regularly assess your marketing efforts through the lens of ROI. What's giving you a meaningful return, and what's draining your energy without results? This doesn't always mean dollars in the bank. ROI might show up as one of these:

- A new podcast interview that brings in consulting leads
- A social media post that sparks a valuable partnership
- A local event that leads to bulk book orders

The key is to identify what's working based on your definition of success. Are you getting closer to your goals? Are certain actions consistently producing high-impact results? ROI isn't just a financial metric but also a sustainability check. It helps you focus on what's actually moving the needle so you can do more of what works and gracefully release what doesn't.

TAKE ACTION
Your Book Marketing Roadmap

A structured book marketing plan prevents overwhelm, keeps you focused, and creates consistent progress over time. Here, in a notebook, or in the online workbook, do the planning that will ultimately become your Strategic Book Marketing Plan. Each section addresses one essential element of the planning stage.

For now, think of your book marketing roadmap as an evolving strategy. Track engagement, refine your approach, and celebrate every milestone.

My Book Buyer List

Your buyer list makes it easy to plan for and track your engagement and outreach strategies. Start by asking yourself, "Who is already in my network that would be thrilled to support my book?" Using this example table below, one of your own, or one from this book's website, create a buyer list based on the three types of book buyers and how they can support your marketing efforts.

To download an editable buyer outreach tracker spreadsheet, visit **promoteyourpurposebook.com/bonuses**.

Buyer Name	Buyer Email	Category	LinkedIn Connection?	Social Media Connection?	Agreed to Purchase Book?	Agreed to Promote Book?	Agreed to Write a Review?

What small steps can you take this week to organize and energize these connections?

My Influencers

Similar to your buyer list, an influencer list helps you track your outreach and relationship-building efforts. But instead of focusing on who will buy your book, this list highlights who will *amplify* it. These are people who can help you reach new audiences, boost your credibility, and generate buzz through their platforms or networks.

Use the following space to begin identifying the influencers who are most aligned with your book's message. Who already has the trust of your target audience? Who shares similar values or goals? Choose two or three people or organizations to start with, and brainstorm how you might begin building or deepening those relationships. Here's an example for inspiration:

Potential Influencer: A local Chamber of Commerce director.

Why They're a Good Fit: They're deeply connected to small business owners and frequently organize speaker series and networking events.

Next Step: Reach out to introduce the book and propose a workshop or talk tied to the book's themes.

Potential Influencer	Why They're a Good Fit	Next Step

PROMOTE YOUR PURPOSE

Keeping track of the potential influencers you've identified will help you stay organized and strategic in your outreach. Use this tracker to record who you've contacted, what you've asked, and how they responded. Whether you're seeking media coverage, testimonials, or event partnerships, this table keeps your momentum moving and your relationships intentional.

To download an editable influencer outreach tracker spreadsheet please visit **promoteyourpurposebook.com/bonuses.**

Influencer Name	Influencer Email	Category	Proximity	Reach/ Audience	Suggested Ask	Ambassador/ Testimonial/ Media	Agreed to Write a Review?

My Plan for Reviews

Book reviews are one of the most powerful tools for visibility and credibility, but only if you're intentional about asking for them. A thoughtful review plan makes it easier to ask for support, track responses, and stay consistent. Think of reviews not as favors, but as ways for your early readers to contribute meaningfully to your message. Here are the steps to take:

1. List Your First Three Reviewers

Who are three people in your network who have read (or will read) your book and would be willing to leave a thoughtful, honest review?

Name	Initial Ask Date	First Follow-Up Date	Second Follow-Up Date

2. Write Your Review Request Template

Draft the message you'll send when asking for a review. Keep it short, appreciative, and clear. Here's an example: "If the book resonated with you, I'd be so grateful if you'd share a review on Amazon. Just a few sentences about what stood out or who you think would benefit from it goes a long way. Here's the link: [Insert URL]."

....

....

....

....

3. Create a Review Reminder System

How will you track who you've asked and follow up gently after one or two weeks?

- ☐ Spreadsheet tracker
- ☐ Calendar reminders
- ☐ CRM system
- ☐ Notes app or project board

My Pre-Order Campaign Plan

A strong pre-order campaign gives your book early traction and creates opportunities to engage with your audience in creative, value-driven ways. Whether you're offering one tier or five, this plan helps you clarify your bonuses, outreach timeline, and fulfillment strategy.

▸ **Pre-Order Start + End Date**

Launch date: ....

Final day to pre-order: ....

When you will start to ship / fulfill bonuses: ....

▸ **List Your Bonus Tiers**

What will you offer at each tier (low, mid, high)?

- ▸ Low-Tier Offer:..
- ▸ Mid-Tier Offer:..
- ▸ High-Tier Offer:...

▸ **Fulfillment Plan**

Who's managing fulfillment?

- ☐ Me
- ☐ My team
- ☐ Third party

Will you ship internationally?

- ☐ Yes
- ☐ No

▸ **Promotion Plan**

Where will you share your pre-order offer?

- ☐ Email list
- ☐ Social media
- ☐ Podcast appearances
- ☐ Partner/affiliate networks
- ☐ Direct outreach to buyers or influencers

▸ **Tracking and Tools**

How will you track orders and supporter info?

- ☐ Google Form
- ☐ Order system on website
- ☐ Crowdfunding platform dashboard
- ☐ Spreadsheet

My Sustainable Approach

Sustainable marketing is about protecting your energy, pacing your efforts, and designing a rhythm that helps you stay visible without burning out. Use this section to define your long-game strategy, and what you'll let go of to stay focused and grounded.

1. Set Your Boundaries

What will you *not* do in your marketing that drains you or distracts you from what matters most? Here are a few examples:

I will not

- check book sales data every day
- compare my launch to that of other authors
- take on more than one marketing task per week

I will pause or delegate

- design tasks (social media graphics, email banners) to a contractor
- pre-order fulfillment to a friend, family member, or VA
- email management for two weeks post-launch so I can rest and recharge.

I will not ....

....

....

I will pause or delegate ....

....

....

PROMOTE YOUR PURPOSE

I will not ....

....

....

I will pause or delegate ....

....

....

I will not ....

....

....

I will pause or delegate ....

....

....

2. Define Your Marketing Rhythms

Choose one to two actions you can do consistently (weekly or monthly) that feel manageable and aligned:

- ☐ Write one blog or newsletter each month
- ☐ Pitch to one podcast or media outlet each week
- ☐ Share a story or review from a reader on social
- ☐ Send quarterly updates to buyers or supporters
- ☐ Other: ....

3. Sustainability Check-In Questions

Use these to evaluate your efforts monthly or quarterly:

	WEEKLY	MONTHLY	QUARTERLY
What's working and still energizing me?			
What's giving me a strong return on time/energy?			
What can I simplify or automate going forward?			

▸ **Design Your Recovery Ritual**

Sustainable marketing includes recovery, which means moments to breathe, reset, or celebrate how far you've come. Instead of waiting until burnout forces you to stop, plan ahead by building in intentional pauses that nourish you.

Step 1: Choose a Milestone to Celebrate

Pick a meaningful point in your book marketing journey when you'll pause to reflect or reward yourself.

- ☐ Finishing pre-order fulfillment
- ☐ Completing your launch event
- ☐ Hitting your first 25 or 100 sales
- ☐ Sending your final launch email
- ☐ Other: ....

Step 2: Design a Recovery Ritual

What would feel truly restorative or celebratory for you?

- ☐ Take a solo creative day (journaling, walking, making art).
- ☐ Treat yourself to something special you wouldn't normally buy.
- ☐ Unplug completely for a day (no marketing, no screens).
- ☐ Finally tackle that cleaning or organizing project you've been putting off.
- ☐ Host a gathering with close friends or supporters.
- ☐ Plan a short trip or nature retreat.
- ☐ Book a spa day or therapy session.
- ☐ Play your favorite music, and really listen.
- ☐ Other: ....

Step 3: Put It on Your Calendar

Don't leave it as a "someday." Book it like you would any other commitment.

Date: ....

Who do I need to notify or involve? (e.g., family, team, coauthor, friends)

....

....

....

....

What needs to be blocked off or rescheduled? (e.g., meetings, marketing tasks, client work) ....

....

....

....

What resources or logistics do I need to plan for? (e.g., budget, transportation, supplies, location) ....
....
....

How will I protect this time and honor it when it arrives? (e.g., setting reminders, enlisting an accountability partner) ....
....
....

Take a step back and look at all you've done. As you review your Strategic Book Marketing Plan, what feels like the clearest next step? What early wins can you prioritize to build momentum from day one? How can you make marketing your book feel more sustainable and energizing rather than overwhelming? What is one system you could set up now to support long-term momentum?

Marketing a book is a long game. The more clearly you plan ahead and track your return on energy, time, money, and attention, the more confident and strategic your future efforts will become. Choose your next step and start building the momentum that will carry you forward.

> **PUT PURPOSE INTO PRACTICE**
>
> Build a marketing plan that reflects your goals, values, and capacity. Focus on cultivating trusted relationships, organizing your outreach, and designing a strategy that supports long-term visibility, not just your launch. Use the tools in this chapter to turn scattered ideas into a clear, actionable path forward.

EXECUTE

CHAPTER 11
Execute Consistently and Create Momentum

PICK YOUR PATH

If you've already executed your Strategic Book Marketing Plan and are now looking to nurture it, skip to chapter 12.

Now that you have your marketing roadmap in place, it's time for the most crucial phase of the ASPEN Method: Execution. Execution is the moment when intentional planning turns into purposeful action. And that's about momentum, not perfection. Whether you're preparing for launch or aiming to sustain your visibility long-term, this chapter will help you implement your strategy with confidence, adapt in real time, and keep your book in front of the readers who need it most.

Just like strategy, execution isn't about doing everything at once but about doing the right things at the right time. And marketing is an ongoing process that requires both structure and adaptability. Strategy in execution helps you stay in control and take consistent action, turning your ideas into lasting visibility, sales, and impact.

In this chapter, we will explore two elements of executing your Strategic Book Marketing Plan:

▸ **Daily, Weekly, and Monthly Execution Tasks for Book Marketing**

　Take action on your marketing roadmap by turning your plan into structured, consistent marketing activities.

- **Executing a Strategic and Powerful Book Launch**

    Build on pre-launch momentum, create an engaging launch day, and sustain long-term visibility.

This phase is where strategy and planning meet action. Whether you're preparing for your book launch or working to maintain momentum, post-launch or otherwise, this chapter will guide you in taking purposeful steps forward.

> ### A Quick Note If Your Book Hasn't Launched Yet
>
> Don't wait to start building momentum. Pre-orders are one of the strongest leveraging strategies available to you. Opening pre-orders early allows you to start promoting your book, building excitement, gathering early reviews, and creating visibility well before your official launch day. Using your marketing roadmap to drive energy toward your pre-order campaign is a powerful way to lay the foundation for a successful launch.

Focus on Real Impact, Not Vanity Metrics

Before you start checking boxes and tracking numbers, let's revisit your mindset about marketing. Take a moment to ask yourself, "What actually matters?"

In a world where social media metrics dominate conversations, it's easy to assume that likes, follows, or viral content are the ultimate signs of success. But these are *vanity metrics*, which means they look good on paper but don't always lead to meaningful results. What matters more is *genuine engagement*, the kinds of actions that reflect trust and connection:

- Replying to your email
- Booking you for a talk or event
- Downloading a bonus resource
- Leaving an intentional review
- Referring you to a friend or colleague

These aren't just numbers. They're signals that your message is resonating. And trust is what turns readers into clients, partners, and advocates.

Mistakes Are Part of the Journey

As you bring your Strategic Book Marketing Plan to life, it's important to remember that no one executes perfectly. Every successful author you admire has behind them marketing mistakes, messy launches, missed opportunities, and posts that didn't land. These aren't signs of failure; they're signs of movement, learning, and resilience.

Perfection isn't the goal. Progress is.

Each time you show up, whether the result is polished or messy, you move your book closer to the people who need it most. Mistakes are not detours; they are the path.

Daily, Weekly, and Monthly Execution Tasks for Book Marketing

Marketing success isn't about one-time efforts; it's about consistent, repeatable actions. With impact and progress in mind, here's how to break down the workload of your Strategic Book Marketing Plan into manageable daily, weekly, and monthly tasks:

Daily Tasks (15–30 Minutes per Day)

These tasks focus on engagement, visibility, and consistent outreach to keep your book top-of-mind. Pick a couple of these tasks to accomplish in a 15–30-minute time block.

Email and Communication

- Respond to reader emails, messages, and inquiries.
- Send follow-ups to previous media, podcast, or collaboration pitches.
- Check in with potential influencers or brand partners to maintain connections.

Social Media and Content Engagement

- Post on one or more aligned social media platforms you enjoy being on.
- Engage with comments, shares, and messages from followers.
- Reshare any reader-generated content, testimonials, or reviews.
- Post an interactive story (poll, question, or quiz) to boost engagement.
- Tag or mention influencers, book clubs, or relevant organizations.

Tracking and Optimization

- Review social media engagement to determine which posts are performing best.
- If applicable, monitor book sales through your publisher, Amazon, Ingram, or your website.
- If you're running paid campaigns on Amazon, Google, or a preferred social media platform, track key ad metrics. (For a quick reference guide on tracking ad metrics, see appendix D.)
- Make notes on what's working and what needs adjustment.

Daily efforts build traction over time and prevent your marketing from feeling overwhelming.

Weekly Tasks (2–3 Hours per Week)

Building from your daily tasks, you can add weekly tasks that focus on bigger marketing actions to drive book sales and brand visibility. Weekly tasks should focus on broader marketing efforts, such as writing email campaigns, pitching podcast hosts, and creating blog or video content. Pick a few of these key tasks and tackle them slowly and steadily.

Email Marketing and Content Creation

- Write and send out a weekly email newsletter. You can feature new reviews, insights, or book-related tips.

- Draft a blog post, contribute an article on your favorite platform, or create a social media post that provides value to your audience.
- Schedule social media posts for the upcoming week to maintain consistency.
- Review and refine your CTAs in emails, social media, and on your website.

Outreach and Visibility

- Pitch yourself to three to five podcast hosts, bloggers, or media outlets for potential interviews or guest articles.
- Contact book clubs, libraries, colleges and universities, or organizations that might be interested in bulk book purchases. (For more on marketing to academic institutions, see appendix E.)
- Engage in meaningful discussions within author communities, online groups, or forums related to your book's topic.
- Follow up with influencers or industry experts who could help amplify your book.

Paid and Organic Marketing Adjustments

- Review and adjust your Amazon, Google, or other ad campaigns (if applicable).
- Check analytics for your website, email, and social media to see which efforts are generating the most engagement.
- Test a new promotional strategy, such as a giveaway, discount, or partnership.

Book Reviews and Endorsements

- Follow up with readers who've purchased the book to ask for reviews on Amazon or Goodreads.
- Identify five to ten more people in your network who could leave a review, and send them a friendly reminder.

> Execution is the moment when intentional planning turns into purposeful action. And that's about momentum, not perfection.

- If someone leaves a great review, screenshot it and share it on social media or in an email campaign.

Weekly efforts ensure steady momentum and keep you connected with new audiences. Keep refining and testing what works.

Monthly Tasks (4–6 Hours per Month)

Monthly tasks focus on big-picture strategy, analysis, and planning for sustained success. They should include larger strategic efforts such as analyzing marketing performance, refining campaigns, and identifying new opportunities for visibility.

Analyze and Optimize Your Marketing Strategy

- Review your sales trends to identify which marketing efforts are driving the most book purchases.
- Assess which social media posts, ads, or email campaigns are performing best.
- Identify areas where you could improve engagement or refine messaging.

New Opportunities and Expanding Your Reach

- Pitch yourself as a speaker for conferences, workshops, or corporate events that align with your book's topic.
- Develop bulk order opportunities with organizations or businesses.
- Research holiday gift lists. (Many of these have long lead times and accept submissions three to six months in advance.)
- Identify relevant literary awards with open submission periods, especially those tied to your genre, subject matter, or identity.
- Participate in book fairs. (For a list of what to bring with you, see appendix F.)
- Check in with any partnerships or collaborations you've been working on.

Long-Term Content and Repurposing

- Identify your best-performing content and repurpose it into new formats, such as turning a blog post into a video or a social post into an email topic.
- Plan out your content calendar for the next month.
- Refresh your Amazon book description, website, or social media bios if needed.

Book Promotion and Seasonal Campaigns

- Plan a seasonal campaign, such as back-to-school incentives, holiday promotions, or summer reading lists.
- Update or create new promotional materials, including bookmarks, postcards, digital graphics, and any other bonus items.
- Offer a limited-time giveaway to encourage purchases and engagement.

Monthly reviews help ensure that your marketing efforts continue evolving. If something isn't working, shift your focus to what's producing results.

Executing a Strategic Book Marketing Plan requires a series of intentional marketing efforts designed to create momentum. So now that you've determined what tasks you need to consider, let's talk about launch day and how to make the most of it.

Executing a Powerful Book Launch

A successful book launch isn't about executing a single event. It's about a series of intentional actions that create momentum, generate excitement, and establish long-term visibility for your book. Whether you're hosting an in-person gathering, a virtual event, or a combination of both, thoughtful execution is key. Your launch should align with your audience, your goals, and the strategy you built in the Planning phase, so each approach offers unique benefits.

Let's bring it all to life so you can build anticipation, engage with your audience, and maximize your book's visibility before, during, and after your book launch.

Clarifying Your Launch Goals

Before diving into specific launch strategies, revisit the goals you set for your book. A successful launch is about aligning your efforts with the bigger vision for your book, not just about selling as many copies as possible on release day. Ask yourself these questions:

- What do I want to accomplish with my book launch?
- Is my primary goal sales, visibility, engagement, or community-building?
- Do I want to connect with existing readers or reach new ones?
- Is media coverage or influencer participation important to me?
- Do I want to generate leads for other parts of my business, such as speaking engagements, consulting, or online courses?

Pick one primary goal and one secondary goal for your launch and write them down. Every launch decision you make should support one of those two outcomes. You can focus on other strategies at a different time in the evolution of your book.

To avoid post-launch disappointment, define what success looks like in measurable terms. Whether it's hitting a specific sales target, making a bestseller list, getting a certain number of reviews, or securing media coverage, having clear benchmarks will guide your efforts and help you celebrate wins along the way.

Your launch strategy should fuel the long-term success of your book, not just generate buzz for one day. Keeping your broader business or career goals in mind will ensure that every effort you make serves a larger purpose. As you execute your launch, don't forget what sets your book apart. That unique angle is more than a detail; it's your story's engine. Use it in your emails, your launch posts, and your interviews. That's what people connect to.

> Want to see how other authors have hosted successful book launches, both online and in person? Visit **promoteyourpurposebook.com/bonuses** to watch our internal video, browse real-world case studies, and get inspired by launch strategies that work across different genres and goals.

PROMOTE YOUR PURPOSE

Defining the Type of Book Launch That Works for You

Once you've set your goals, the next step is to determine what kind of book launch event best fits your needs. Your book launch can take place in many forms, and in many cases a combination of online and offline events creates the most well-rounded approach.

While some authors prefer an intimate in-person event, others leverage the accessibility and reach of virtual launches. When a PYP author launched her book, for instance, she hosted a 20-minute Instagram Live Q&A instead of a formal launch party. That one event drove 60 percent of her first-week sales, and she repurposed the video for weeks after launch. This worked for her because she had a large following and had been nurturing her audience for months leading up to this day.

You can also plan multiple events that cater to different segments of your audience. There are two primary options:

1. Virtual Book Launch

A virtual book launch is a great way to engage readers from anywhere, create shareable content, and reach people who may not be able to attend an in-person event. Here are some ways to create a virtual launch event.

- **Host a Live Q&A or Reading**

    Whether on Zoom, Instagram Live, or LinkedIn, interacting with your audience in real time allows you to share the inspiration behind your book, read an excerpt, and answer reader questions. Having a moderator to facilitate the conversation can keep the event structured and engaging.

- **Leverage Social Media Countdown and Engagement**

    In the days leading up to your launch, build excitement by sharing behind-the-scenes content, teaser quotes, or a countdown. On launch day, encourage your audience to post photos with your book and tag you.

- **Partner with Online Communities**

  Whether through a virtual book club, guest appearances in online groups, or collaborations with influencers, tapping into existing communities can expand your reach beyond your immediate network.

- **Encourage Early Reviews**

  Ask your launch team, beta readers, and close supporters to leave early reviews on Amazon and Goodreads. Even if readers purchase from other retailers, reviews on these sites play a major role in how potential buyers evaluate books.

2. In-Person Book Launch

An in-person book launch allows you to connect directly with readers, sign books, and create a memorable experience. Consider the scale and format that best fits your audience and your personal style.

- **Host an Intimate Gathering**

  A private launch party with friends, family, and supporters can serve as a meaningful celebration of your achievement. You can host it in your home, a bookstore, or a local venue.

- **Plan a Public Event**

  Whether at a bookstore, library, or conference, a public event provides an opportunity to introduce your book to new readers. If your book ties into a specific industry, consider launching at a relevant professional event where your target audience is already gathered.

- **Tying Your Launch Into an Existing Event**

  Rather than planning an entirely new event, look for opportunities to integrate your launch into something that's already happening, such as a conference, corporate gathering, or community event. This reduces logistic challenges while ensuring a built-in audience.

- **Sponsorships and Partnerships**

    If you're hosting a large-scale event, consider securing sponsors to cover venue costs, catering, or marketing expenses. Businesses and organizations that align with your book's topic may be willing to support your event in exchange for visibility.

One-Page Sell Sheets and Launch Tool Kits

As part of your launch preparation, consider creating a one-page sell sheet for your book. This is a versatile tool that can be used when pitching yourself for speaking engagements, sending outreach to organizations for bulk sales, or following up after a conference or podcast appearance.

> Looking for a ready-made template to start with? Access the customizable template at **promoteyourpurposebook.com/bonuses**.

Think of your one-pager as a snapshot of your book's value and positioning. It should be easy to scan, professionally designed, and aligned with your book's branding or your overall company branding to make your book (and you) easy to say yes to. A great one-pager includes the following:

- Your book title, subtitle, and a short description
- A brief author bio with your headshot
- Who the book is for and what it helps them do
- Key endorsements or reviews
- Ordering details, including bulk or discounted options
- Contact information and relevant links

You can use a one-pager in digital outreach as a PDF attachment, or you can print hard copies to hand out at events.

> A successful book launch isn't about executing a single event. It's about a series of intentional actions that create momentum, generate excitement, and establish long-term visibility for your book.

Building Pre-Launch Momentum

The weeks leading up to your launch set the stage for success. This is when you ramp up anticipation, engage your audience, and ensure that every logistic detail is in place.

- Start by reaching out to your email list with a countdown series that reminds subscribers of the upcoming release. Use these emails to share behind-the-scenes insights, highlight testimonials, and offer exclusive bonuses for early buyers.
- On social media, increase engagement by posting teaser excerpts, behind-the-scenes content, and countdown graphics.
- If you've scheduled media interviews, podcast appearances, or guest articles, confirm dates, provide final promotional materials, and make sure your messaging aligns with your book's overall marketing plan.
- If your book isn't at the launch phase yet, you can ask your audience for input on your title, subtitle, and cover design as a way to begin pre-launch momentum.
- It's also crucial to test your sales links and event setup. If your marketing plan includes having your book available through multiple platforms, double-check purchase links, verify order processing, and ensure everything is working smoothly. If you're hosting a virtual launch event, test your Zoom or streaming platform in advance to avoid any last-minute technical issues.

If engagement is lower than expected, consider adding interactive elements such as a live Q&A session, an exclusive giveaway, or a limited-time offer to increase participation. Whichever strategy you use, your goal is to make sure people are excited and ready to take action when your book becomes available.

Making the Most of Launch Day

Launch day isn't about perfection; it's about connection. Show up fully, celebrate your readers, and make it easy for them to celebrate you. If something goes wrong, remember that being human is part of what makes your launch meaningful. Your book's release is a moment worth celebrating, but more importantly it's an opportunity to drive engagement and sales in a concentrated timeframe. Instead of trying to do everything, focus on a few high-impact actions that amplify your message and make it easy for others to support you.

- **Start with a Dedicated Launch Email**

    An initial launch email should be simple, clear, and compelling. Announce that your book is officially available, thank your community for their support, and include a direct link to purchase. Don't overcomplicate it. A short, heartfelt message with one strong CTA is all you need. (For real examples you can adapt, see appendix G.) If your email list is small or you're just getting started, don't worry. This isn't about numbers but about activating the people who already believe in your message. Even a handful of engaged readers can help spread the word far and wide.

- **Go Live on Social Media to Celebrate with Your Audience**

    Share your excitement, thank your supporters, and offer a quick behind-the-scenes story about your journey. A few minutes of genuine enthusiasm can go a long way in helping your audience feel like they're part of something special.

- **Ask for Early Reviews**

    Verified Amazon reviews are critical for long-term visibility, so make it easy for your supporters to leave one. Provide a direct review link and a quick prompt, such as "What's one thing you took away from the book?" or "Why would you recommend this to a friend?"

▸ **Stay Present and Responsive**

Throughout the day, stay actively engaged. Respond to social media comments, answer emails, and thank people for their support. If you notice engagement is slower than expected, try a midday reminder announcing a special bonus or incentive to reenergize your audience and keep the momentum going. If things feel quieter than expected, know that that's normal. Keep showing up. You can always send a second message or post later in the day with a fun incentive, such as a behind-the-scenes video, a giveaway entry, or a limited-time bonus for anyone who purchases that day.

This is your moment, but it's not your only one. Launch day is the spark, not the whole fire. Celebrate what you've accomplished, keep showing up, and trust that your impact will continue to grow.

Keeping the Momentum Going Post-Launch

Your launch day is just the beginning. Many books see an initial spike in sales, followed by a drop-off in visibility, and many authors feel immense pressure to pick the *perfect* launch day, as if everything hinges on that single moment. But here's the truth: Your book doesn't have to explode on day one to be successful. It can simmer and grow. Sustainable promotion means building long-term momentum, not chasing a fleeting spike. As one author I worked with shared, "I thought I had to hit a specific date, but Jenn reminded me it's about steady visibility, not rushing the process." When you give your launch timeline room to flex, you protect your energy and often create more meaningful impact over time.

The key to sustaining success is having a post-launch strategy in place. Here are some elements to consider executing:

▸ **Reengage Your Audience**

Plan another wave of marketing two to four weeks after your initial launch. Continue highlighting reader testimonials, media coverage, and any new milestones your book achieves. If you hosted a launch event, you can repurpose the content, using video clips, testimonials, and photos to keep the conversation going.

- **Prioritize Review Requests**

    Keep reminding readers that their feedback is invaluable and makes a meaningful impact. Personalized follow-ups, email reminders, and social media shout-outs can encourage more people to leave reviews.

- **Keep Pitching**

    If you haven't already, pitch your book to additional media outlets, podcasts, and influencers. Even after launch, many platforms are open to featuring new books, especially if you present a compelling reason their audience would benefit from your content.

- **Relaunch with Purpose**

    To maintain long-term interest, consider hosting a second book launch event a few months after your book's initial release. Position it as a "book tour stop," an "anniversary celebration," or an "exclusive Q&A session" with new insights from the book.

But don't stop there. Think beyond launch events. Your book can become the foundation of an ongoing movement. Instead of treating your marketing like a one-time campaign, build a container for your readers to stay engaged, such as a monthly Zoom circle, an email sequence, a LinkedIn group, or a branded series that keeps your purpose front and center.

People want more than something to buy. They want something to belong to.

> People want more than something to buy. They want something to belong to.

EXECUTE CONSISTENTLY AND CREATE MOMENTUM

TAKE ACTION
From Planning to Executing

Marketing your book doesn't stop after launch. It's a continuous process of engagement, visibility, and refinement. A strong Execution phase sets the stage, but long-term success comes from maintaining momentum and nurturing your audience over time.

Before you lay out your daily, weekly, and monthly tasks, start by revisiting your marketing roadmap from the Planning phase. Break down your major milestones into smaller, actionable steps that will move the needle forward. Remember to make them SMART goals. Saying, "I want media coverage" isn't enough. You need to outline the specific actions that will make it happen. Whether it's a daily checklist or a structured campaign calendar, having a system in place keeps you organized and ensures your marketing efforts stay on course.

Now, use these prompts to guide your thinking and track your progress. Whether you're using this space, a notebook, the online workbook, a spreadsheet, or a project management tool, what matters most is creating a system that works for you. Map your marketing rhythm to design a structure that fits your bandwidth and goals.

My Daily, Weekly, and Monthly Tasks

The Execution phase is about implementing your marketing strategies with precision and adaptability. So instead of waiting for everything to be perfect, focus on small, consistent actions that align with your larger marketing goals. Start by jotting down one to three low-effort actions you can do daily in each category. Daily tasks foster your connections, so they should focus on engagement, visibility, and consistent outreach that can be refined or expanded over time. Here are some examples:

PROMOTE YOUR PURPOSE

- **Task Type: Show Up on Social Media**
  Daily Action: Post a quote, tip, or behind-the-scenes photo such as signing books on LinkedIn.

- **Task Type: Engage with My Audience**
  Daily Action: Reply to DMs, comments, or reader emails.

- **Task Type: Track and Optimize**
  Daily Action: Monitor post performance or jot down what's getting the most engagement.

- **Task Type: Say Thank You**
  Daily Action: Send a personal thank-you note or tag a supporter.

TASK TYPE	DAILY ACTION(S)
Show Up on Social Media	
Engage with My Audience	
Track and Optimize	
Say Thank You	

Weekly tasks should be focused on bigger marketing actions, such as writing email campaigns, pitching podcast hosts, and creating blog or video content. Staying consistent is key, but that doesn't mean you need to do everything at once. Pick a few tasks in each category that you'll tackle slowly and steadily each week.

TASK TYPE	WEEKLY ACTION(S)
Marketing and Content Creation	
Outreach and Visibility	
Refinements	
Reviews and Endorsements	
Say Thank You	

PROMOTE YOUR PURPOSE

Now, turn your focus to monthly tasks, the big-picture strategies and efforts that will help you sustain success. Whether it's leveraging media appearances, securing ongoing book reviews, or running targeted promotional campaigns, each action contributes to your book's long-term relevance, so focus on strategies that feel aligned with your goals and bandwidth.

TASK TYPE	MONTHLY ACTION(S)
Analyze and Optimize	
New Opportunities	
Content Repurposing	
Promotions and Campaigns	
Say Thank You	

EXECUTE CONSISTENTLY AND CREATE MOMENTUM

Your Book Launch, Your Way

There is no one-size-fits-all approach to launch a book. Some authors opt for a quiet, intimate gathering, while others host high-energy public events. What matters most is that your launch feels meaningful to you and aligns with the goals you've set for your book. Whatever format you choose, stay connected with your readers, celebrate your success, and enjoy the moment. This is only the beginning of your book's journey.

1. Define Your Launch Vision

My primary goal for launch is (e.g., visibility, reviews, community connection, bulk orders, leads): ....

....

....

....

My secondary goal for launch is: ....

....

....

....

Success will look like (e.g., 25 reviews in the first month, 100 pre-orders, three speaking invites): ....

....

....

....

PROMOTE YOUR PURPOSE

2. Choose Your Top Three Launch Activities

Pick the activities that feel exciting, sustainable, or aligned with your audience. Check them here.

Options to consider:

- ☐ In-person event
- ☐ Virtual launch (Zoom, Instagram, LinkedIn Live)
- ☐ Media or podcast tour
- ☐ Live reading or Q&A
- ☐ Social media countdown
- ☐ Bonus offer or giveaway
- ☐ LinkedIn article series
- ☐ Newsletter launch series
- ☐ Partnership or sponsored event

Prioritize Your Top Three Picks:

1 ....

2 ....

3 ....

3. Celebrate the Moment

Even a soft launch deserves celebration. Mark the moment your book goes live in a way that honors the work you've done.

I will celebrate launch day by: ....

....

....

....

Optional add-ons:
- Share a gratitude post.
- Host a toast with friends or family.
- Take a solo walk or personal retreat.
- Order a favorite meal.
- Play a launch day anthem.

4. Have a Backup Plan

Things don't always go as planned, and that's okay. Write down a few simple pivots you can turn to if engagement is low, tech fails, or your energy dips.

IF engagement is slower than expected, THEN I will (e.g., resend my launch email, post a giveaway, go live that evening):

....

....

IF I feel discouraged, THEN I will:

....

....

5. Launch Day Checklist

Use this as a quick reference when the big day arrives:

- [ ] Launch email is written and scheduled
- [ ] Social media post(s) is drafted
- [ ] Bonus or giveaway materials are prepped
- [ ] Book links are double-checked
- [ ] Event tech is tested (if virtual)
- [ ] My calendar is blocked to stay present and engaged

PROMOTE YOUR PURPOSE

☐ Support crew or moderator is confirmed

☐ Space is made to enjoy the moment

Again, you don't need to do everything at once. Separating your pre-order period, book delivery date, and celebration events into staggered phases can make the entire launch feel more manageable, especially for memoirists or anyone juggling health needs, caregiving, or other life demands. A soft launch (with digital or pre-order access) followed by a hard launch (when books are in hand or events are scheduled) allows you to build momentum gradually, rather than forcing everything into one high-pressure window. Giving yourself that flexibility isn't just strategic, it's sustainable.

Marketing isn't a one-time push. It's a rhythm. Small, consistent actions taken daily, weekly, and monthly build momentum far more powerfully than sporadic bursts of promotion. By executing with intention and sustaining engagement over time, your book will continue reaching new audiences and creating opportunities long after launch day.

Now take action. Your spotlight is waiting!

> Big results start with small, intentional steps. As you step into Execution, ask yourself these questions:
>
>
>
> **PUT PURPOSE INTO PRACTICE**
>
> ✓ What is one small, specific action I can complete today to move my marketing forward?
>
> ✓ How can I make taking action feel lighter, simpler, and more joyful?
>
> ✓ Where can I give myself permission to start messy and refine as I go?
>
> ✓ Momentum builds when you move forward, even imperfectly. Just begin. Your readers are waiting. Don't hold back!

> Perfection isn't the goal. Progress is.

NURTURE

CHAPTER 12

Nurture Your Book's Impact for Years to Come

PICK YOUR PATH

If you've already determined how you'll nurture your book's impact, skip to appendix A.

Now that you've executed your marketing and book launch strategy, it's time to shift from sprinting to sustaining, using the Nurture phase of the ASPEN Method.

Authors often assume that once their book is launched, their marketing efforts are complete. However, the most successful books don't just experience a short-lived surge of excitement; they remain in circulation, generating engagement, sales, and opportunities for years. Sustained engagement is the key to keeping your book relevant long after its initial release.

In this chapter, we will explore four main ways to nurture your book's success:

- **How to Keep Getting Reviews Over Time**

  Learn how to keep generating reviews long after your launch, using touchpoints such as email follow-ups, reader reminders, and community engagement to maintain visibility and credibility.

- **Keeping the Message Alive Through Content Repurposing**

  Discover how to turn your existing content, such as blog posts, talks, podcast interviews, and social posts, into evergreen marketing tools that keep your message circulating and your workload manageable.

- **Maintaining Reader Engagement and Activity**

    Explore how to deepen relationships with your audience by inviting them into your ecosystem through emails, events, perks, or community spaces so that they continue connecting with your book and your brand.

- **Avoiding Burnout and Staying Consistent**

    Build a sustainable rhythm that protects your energy, prevents overwhelm, and helps you keep showing up with impact, even when life gets busy or your focus shifts.

This phase ensures your book doesn't just make an initial splash but keeps creating impact, opportunities, and connections over time. Whether through reader engagement, media exposure, speaking engagements, or other ongoing efforts, nurturing your marketing strategies means your book will remain visible and valuable and continuously work for you.

Your Legacy Lives Beyond Your Book

Becky Robinson, author of *Reach: Create the Biggest Possible Audience for Your Message, Book, or Cause*, reminds us to think of a book as a seed. During a PYP session for authors, she said, "The more you share it, the more likely it is to do the good work you wrote it to do." Nurturing your message over time is what allows it to grow roots, bear fruit, and reach the people who need it most.

Building a strong relationship with your readers extends beyond selling copies. It's about creating a community of advocates who leave reviews, recommend your book, and engage with your future projects. By continuing to nurture engagement, you transform your book from a one-time purchase into a community-driven movement. This requires a mix of reader interaction, content repurposing, and ongoing engagement strategies to keep your book in your readers' world. To accomplish this, you need consistent touchpoints, valuable interactions, and a structured ecosystem that keeps readers coming back for more.

> Nurturing your message over time is what allows it to grow roots, bear fruit, and reach the people who need it most.

Getting Reviews Over Time

Reviews are one of the most powerful marketing tools available to authors and are crucial for long-term book success. They not only build social proof but also directly impact how platforms such as Amazon rank and recommend your book. A steady stream of new reviews coming in long after your book's launch shows continued interest and relevance, which can help keep your book visible in algorithms and recommendation engines. Whether someone is hearing about your book for the first time or considering whether to recommend it to a friend, reviews play a pivotal role in their decision-making process. Reviews also influence word-of-mouth promotion, arguably the most effective (and most trusted) form of marketing.

Keep the Momentum Going

The initial wave of reviews around launch day is important, but long-term success relies on what's called a long-tail strategy. This means intentionally sustaining visibility and sales well after your official launch through smaller, ongoing efforts that compound over time. Rather than focusing on only a single launch window, you're building a foundation for steady interest, continued engagement, and consistent sales across weeks, months, or even years. Here's how to keep the momentum going:

- **Follow up with early buyers.** Don't assume readers will leave reviews without a nudge. A simple follow-up email can make all the difference.

- **Make it easy to review.** Provide clear instructions and direct links to review pages on Amazon and Goodreads.

- **Engage book clubs and niche communities.** Offer to attend their meetings or provide discussion guides in exchange for feedback and reviews.

- **Leverage podcast and media features.** After guest appearances, direct listeners toward leaving a review if they've read or plan to read your book.

Encourage Reader-Generated Content

Readers who feel connected to your message often want to share it. Encourage them to do so by making it easy and fun:

- Ask them to post a photo of the book with a branded hashtag.
- Highlight reader testimonials on your social media and website.
- Run giveaways that reward creative reader posts or video reviews.
- Use powerful reader quotes in future marketing materials.
- Acknowledge and thank readers who engage. Your response builds loyalty and encourages further sharing.

How can you invite your readers to celebrate and share your book this month, whether through photos, testimonials, creative posts, or otherwise?

Encourage Readers to Revisit Content in New Ways

Just because a reader finishes your book doesn't mean their journey with you is over. Give them reasons to return to your content in different ways by embedding opportunities for further engagement throughout your book. Strategically embedded resources in your book keep readers coming back, allowing you to guide them toward deeper learning, community participation, and additional resources that complement the material in your book.

One of the most effective ways to achieve this is by strategically integrating end-of-chapter resources. In *Publish Your Purpose*, for instance, I played off part of the subtitle, "Grow Your Big Idea," and created a "Grow Further" section at the end of each chapter, where I encouraged readers to download blueprints, watch videos, or join interactive workshops. These additional resources not only enhanced their learning experience but also brought them into my larger ecosystem, keeping them engaged beyond just reading the book. You may have noticed that I've been doing this throughout this entire book as well, which brings me to my next point.

Repurposing Content: Keep the Message Alive

Your book's themes don't have to stay confined to its pages. In fact, if your message is truly meant to create long-term impact, you need to find ways to keep it alive in the minds—and hands—of your audience. Repurposing content is a smart and sustainable way to reinforce key takeaways and meet your readers where they already are, whether that's their inbox, social feed, or favorite podcast app. When you breathe new life into your existing material, you not only expand your reach but also deepen your relationship with your audience by showing up consistently with value that matters.

How I Structured Engagement

In my book *Publish Your Purpose*, I incorporated two popular PDFs available on the PYP website (the Book Cost Blueprint and 9 Questions to Ask a Publisher[12]) directly into the book itself. I then linked to downloadable versions online, which drove engagement beyond the book itself. I didn't just mention additional resources in passing. I embedded them intentionally throughout the book so that every chapter had a clear next step.

Here's how I structured it:

- In the introduction, I encouraged readers to download the companion workbook, providing an interactive way to track their progress.

- Chapters 1–4 directed readers to the Publish Your Purpose Author Lab workshop[13], reinforcing key concepts with video content and exercises.

- Chapters 5–10 led to the 30-Day Book Writing Challenge[14], designed to help readers implement writing strategies in a structured, actionable way.

---

12. https://publishyourpurpose.com/questions-ask-publisher/
13. https://publishyourpurpose.com/author-lab/
14. https://publishyourpurpose.com/30-day-book-writing-challenge/

- Chapter 11 introduced the Pick Your Path to Publishing Webinar[15], giving readers insights into different publishing options before they needed to make a decision.
- Chapters 12–13 encouraged readers to download the 9 Questions to Ask a Publisher blueprint, providing them with a concrete tool to evaluate publishing partners.
- Chapter 14 reintroduced the Pick Your Path to Publishing Webinar, offering additional guidance on selecting the best publishing model.
- Chapter 15 once again pointed readers toward the 9 Questions to Ask a Publisher blueprint, reinforcing the importance of making an informed publishing decision.
- Chapter 16 introduced the Book Cost Blueprint, helping readers understand the financial investment of publishing.
- Chapter 17 brought readers back to the companion workbook, ensuring they had a structured way to apply everything they'd learned.

Think about how you can structure your own chapters to guide readers to new experiences or content. These touchpoints help readers continue engaging with you long after they finish the final page.

There's no real concern about how many times you do this. If you approach this from the mindset of serving your readers rather than being overtly salesy, your readers will appreciate what you've done. Keep in mind that it can take seeing many CTAs before a reader will take action.

Repurpose Content Across Multiple Platforms

Once your repurposed content is strategically placed, it becomes the foundation for email marketing, exclusive reader perks, and long-term visibility. Maximizing your book's reach by sharing its message in different formats keeps your content alive and makes it easier to maintain visibility over time. Here are some common ways authors do this.

---

15. https://publishyourpurpose.com/path-publishing-webinar/

- **Blog Posts → Book Chapters**

  If you have existing articles or blog posts, refine and expand them into full book sections.

- **Book Chapters → Blog Posts**

  Take key excerpts from your book and turn them into blog posts, linking back to the book for deeper insights.

- **Social Media Posts → Key Insights**

  Pull short snippets, quotes, or lessons from your book to create engaging social media content.

- **Webinars or Talks → Book Content**

  If you've given a talk or hosted a webinar on a topic, transcribe it and adapt the insights into a book chapter or bonus material.

- **Podcast Interviews → Marketing Content**

  If you've been featured on a podcast discussing your book's themes, turn that conversation into an article or downloadable resource.

Each format feeds into the next, creating a continuous marketing loop. Which existing piece of content could you repurpose into a new article, video, or resource this month?

Keeping Readers Engaged and Active

Repurposing content ensures your book's message extends beyond its pages by keeping readers engaged across multiple platforms. But once you've identified and strategically placed this content, the next step is to build direct and lasting connections with your audience. By leveraging tools such as email marketing, exclusive perks, and interactive communities, you can transform passive readers into engaged advocates who continue to interact with your book and brand long after their initial read.

> Every resource you offer should guide readers toward your broader ecosystem of content and services.

If your book has an audiobook edition, that connection runs even deeper. As Tina Dietz, founder and CEO of Twin Flames Studios, explains, "When you're thinking about getting your voice out into the world through an audiobook, you're creating a body of work—your voice, your message—four to eight hours of it. That kind of intimate listening creates a deep relationship. It's a visceral way for people to trust you, to get to know you, and to keep your message alive."[16]

Use Your Book to Drive Readers to Your Website

Your book can become a powerful lead-generation tool that guides readers toward deeper engagement. Consider embedding links or QR codes throughout your book that direct readers to one or more of these:

- ▸ Bonus resources or downloads
- ▸ Expanded content or blog posts
- ▸ Free trainings, videos, or masterclasses
- ▸ A place to join your email list

Every resource you offer should guide readers toward your broader ecosystem of content and services. For example, if your book includes a chapter on marketing strategy, you might reference a free marketing checklist available on your website. Your book introduces the concept, but your website provides a deeper dive that keeps your readers engaged with your content long after they've finished the book.

Email List Growth: Keep the Conversation Going

Your email list is one of the most powerful tools for long-term engagement because it allows you to communicate directly with your readers, free from social media algorithms. Unlike social media platforms, where algorithms control who sees your content, your email list guarantees your message reaches people who've already expressed interest in your book.

---

16. Publish Your Purpose, "The Present and Future of Audiobooks with Special Guest, Tina Dietz," YouTube, August 22, 2024, https://www.youtube.com/live/vkpL32iEiFA.

To build and maintain an engaged list, follow this path:

- **Offer Incentives**

    Start by offering an incentive for signing up, such as a free downloadable resource. This could be a worksheet, checklist, or template pulled directly from your book and repackaged as a valuable tool.

- **Introduce and Deliver**

    Once readers have joined, introduce them to your book's key themes while delivering additional insight through an automated follow-up sequence. For instance, repurpose book excerpts into a five-part email series, breaking down important lessons into digestible emails that reinforce your core message over time. (To see an example of my follow-up sequence for *Publish Your Purpose*, please visit promoteyourpurposebook.com/bonuses.)

- **Incorporate Content**

    To add further value, consider incorporating deleted chapters, extended case studies, or behind-the-scenes stories into your regular newsletters. This keeps your book's themes alive while offering fresh perspectives readers won't find elsewhere.

- **Foster Interaction**

    Beyond delivering content, focus on encouraging interaction. Instead of treating emails as one-way communication, end each message with a question or a call to action, such as asking readers to reply with their thoughts, feedback, or experiences. This transforms your audience from passive readers into active community members. If your book includes a section on mindset shifts for success, for example, turn each shift into a separate email, adding personal anecdotes or exercises to help readers apply the concept to their own lives.

By integrating repurposed materials into your email strategy, you're not just keeping your book alive, you're fostering a dynamic ecosystem in which your content continues to resonate and evolve long after launch day.

What's one simple email you could send this week to reengage your readers and invite them deeper into your world?

Exclusive Reader Perks: Rewarding Engagement

Readers love feeling like insiders, and exclusive perks help deepen their connection with you and your book. These incentives enhance engagement while also encouraging word-of-mouth promotion, one of the most effective ways to sustain book sales. Here are a few types of reader perks you can offer:

- **Private Online Spaces**

    Create a dedicated space for your readers to engage with you and each other, such as an online group, Slack channel, Substack, or Patreon community. These spaces encourage ongoing discussions and foster belonging.

- **Live Q&A Sessions**

    Q&A sessions are ideal for nurturing long-term engagement. Hosting monthly or quarterly Zoom calls, Instagram Lives, LinkedIn events, or YouTube live streams gives readers a chance to connect with you directly, ask questions, and explore your book's themes in a deeper way. These sessions also surface valuable feedback and ideas, helping you stay connected to what resonates most with your audience.

- **Bonus Content**

    Offer deleted chapters, extended case studies, or behind-the-scenes videos. These feel like "insider access" to your creative process.

- **Interactive Challenges or Prompts**

  Run monthly challenges related to your book's topic. For example, if your book covers leadership, you could offer a "Leadership in Action" challenge and invite readers to report back.

- **Early Access and Sneak Peeks**

  Reward loyal readers with early access to your next project, a beta reader opportunity, or an exclusive sneak peek of what's coming next.

What small "insider" experience could you offer to your most loyal readers?

Community and Interaction: Creating Spaces for Connection

Readers don't just buy books; they invest in ideas, experiences, and connections. Your book is a gateway to deeper engagement. By fostering a community around it, you keep readers engaged, loyal, and eager to share your work.

- **Reader Discussions**

  Encouraging reader discussions is a simple way to spark engagement. Start conversations on social media, email newsletters, or blog posts, asking thought-provoking questions that relate to your book's core message.

- **Book Clubs**

  Joining book clubs that feature your book is another way to stay connected with your readers. Offering to attend virtual or in-person book club meetings as a guest author can create a personal connection and deepen engagement.

- **Virtual Events**

  Hosting virtual events is another way to create an interactive experience. Whether it's a webinar, AMA (Ask Me Anything) session, or a live panel discussion, these events give readers direct access to you while reinforcing your book's message.

- **Public Relations**

    Don't overlook traditional public relations as a powerful engagement tool to spark conversations. When you're featured in an article, quoted in a piece, or profiled by a media outlet, share that coverage with your readers. Let them see the real-world relevance of your message. Use email newsletters, social media, or blog posts to highlight key takeaways from the piece and invite your community to reflect or respond. A short Q&A based on the article topic or a live discussion can deepen the conversation and build momentum around your message.

- **Podcast Appearances**

    As community touchpoints, podcast interviews are a unique opportunity to connect on a more personal, conversational level. When you're a guest on a podcast, share the episode with your audience, along with a few questions or insights to get people thinking. Encourage listeners to comment, reply, or message you with their takeaways. You could even host a follow-up live session to explore the episode's topic in more depth. Each podcast is a fresh invitation for your readers to interact with your ideas and keep the dialogue going.

Remember: Engagement doesn't always have to be large-scale. Personalized interactions can make a big impact. Taking the time to respond to comments, emails, and social media messages shows readers you value their support. A simple thank-you message to someone who leaves a review or a personal reply to a thoughtful question can turn a casual reader into a lifelong fan.

> Consistency isn't about doing everything. It's about doing what matters most, one step at a time.

Avoiding Book Marketing Burnout and Staying Consistent

Book marketing is an ongoing process that requires sustained effort to keep your book relevant and discoverable. Many authors start with excitement and high energy, only to find themselves exhausted trying to maintain momentum over time. The reality is that book marketing is a long game, and without a sustainable approach, it's easy to burn out.

Rather than viewing book promotion as an intense, short-term effort, think of it as a steady rhythm of consistent, manageable actions. Instead of trying to do everything at once, focus on small, intentional marketing strategies that fit into your lifestyle and business goals. Whether you're actively promoting your book every day or dedicating time to it only a few times a month, what matters most is consistency over time.

How to Sustain Book Promotion Without Overwhelm

One of the biggest contributors to book marketing burnout is unrealistic expectations. Many authors believe that if they put in a strong push during their launch, their book will continue selling on its own. However, books remain successful only when authors actively engage with their audiences, continue sharing their messages, and find strategic ways to market their books without constantly creating something new.

It's important to find a book marketing rhythm that aligns with your lifestyle. Even if you can dedicate only one hour per week to promoting your book, use that time strategically. Marketing is about focusing on high-impact actions that build momentum over time.

How to Stay Motivated and Consistent

Balancing book promotion with other responsibilities can feel overwhelming, but by implementing smart systems and shifting your mindset, you can maintain momentum without burning out. Here are some ways that have proven effective:

- **Automate and Schedule Content**

    Use scheduling tools to plan and automate social media posts, emails, and blog updates. This prevents the pressure of daily posting while ensuring consistent visibility.

- **Batch Similar Tasks for Efficiency**

    Instead of marketing your book every single day, set aside a few hours each month to create and schedule content in advance. You can write multiple blog posts, record short video clips, or create promotional graphics in one sitting and distribute them over time.

- **Set Realistic Expectations**

    Book marketing is a long-term investment. Most books don't reach their peak sales within the first month. Focus on maintaining visibility and consistent outreach rather than chasing overnight success.

- **Celebrate Small Wins**

    Whether it's a new review, a social media share, or a podcast invitation, every milestone is a step toward long-term success. Recognizing progress, even in small ways, helps maintain motivation and momentum.

Avoiding burnout isn't about stopping book promotion but about making it sustainable. By focusing on automation, repurposing content, and setting realistic expectations, you can keep your book in the conversation without feeling overwhelmed.

> The true heart of purpose-driven work is knowing that your influence doesn't end with you but lives on in the people, communities, and movements you touch.

NURTURE YOUR BOOK'S IMPACT FOR YEARS TO COME

TAKE ACTION
Sustain the Spark

Now that your book is out in the world, it's time to shift from launching to lasting impact. The Nurture phase of the ASPEN Method isn't about pushing harder but about showing up smarter. This is where your message keeps working for you over time through intentional choices that build momentum, deepen reader relationships, and protect your energy.

Use these prompts and strategies to begin building the final piece of your Strategic Book Marketing Plan. These activities are designed to help you nurture engagement consistently and sustainably. Record your answers in the space provided, a notebook, or in the online workbook, which includes additional worksheets and templates to help you stay organized and aligned.

Nurture My Reviews

A steady stream of reviews keeps your book visible and credible long after launch day. Plan how you'll continue generating reviews over time, not just through big campaigns, but through everyday touchpoints.

Who are five people you haven't yet asked for a review but could?

1. ....
2. ....
3. ....
4. ....
5. ....

245

PROMOTE YOUR PURPOSE

What follow-up message could you send to readers or event attendees to encourage a review?

....

....

....

....

....

....

Where have you or can you share a direct review link for your book? (Check all that apply)

- ☐ Email signature
- ☐ Website (book page, thank-you page, etc.)
- ☐ Post-purchase thank-you email
- ☐ Newsletter or welcome email series
- ☐ Social media bio (Instagram, LinkedIn, etc.)
- ☐ Social media posts or stories
- ☐ Podcast show notes or outro
- ☐ Inside the book (QR code or short link)
- ☐ Other ....

Create a simple one-liner CTA to use consistently. Example: "If this book helped you, would you leave a quick review? It makes a huge difference."

....

....

Repurpose My Content

Sustainable book marketing and promotion starts with one intentional step. Your story didn't end when you finished writing your book. It's only just beginning.

Take a structured approach by mapping out your book's core sections and identifying where existing content—blog posts, videos, blueprints, checklists, social media posts, or podcast appearances—can fit into your engagement strategy. Think of it like a puzzle, and start by asking yourself, "What content have I already created that supports my book's themes? Where can it be adapted for new formats or deeper engagement?"

Step 1: Choose one key theme from your book.

Example: Overcoming self-doubt as a first-time entrepreneur

Theme: ....

Step 2: Identify one existing asset that supports this theme (e.g., blog post, podcast episode, video, workshop, slide deck)

Example: Blog post titled "Why Imposter Syndrome Hits New Business Owners the Hardest"

Existing content: ....

Step 3: Decide how to repurpose it for a new format or audience.

Examples:

Turn my blog into an article for LinkedIn.

Use my workshop to create a three-part email series.

New format or platform: ....

Step 4: Plan your next action step.

Example: Pull three key quotes from the blog and design a workshop presentation for next Tuesday.

PROMOTE YOUR PURPOSE

What I will do next: ....

Now go share it and shape the future you're here to create.

Foster Long-Term Engagement

Once someone finishes your book, what keeps them in your world? Use this space to design a reader experience that keeps the connection alive.

What's one logical next step a reader could take after finishing your book? (e.g., download a resource, join your list, attend a live event)

....
....
....
....

What existing touchpoint could you strengthen or make more inviting?

....
....
....
....

What new opportunity or community space could you introduce this quarter?

....
....
....
....

NURTURE YOUR BOOK'S IMPACT FOR YEARS TO COME

Now, map your reader's journey. What are three to five touchpoints between "Purchase my book" and "Become an active community member"?

1. ....
2. ....
3. ....
4. ....
5. ....

Avoid Burnout

Consistent book marketing doesn't mean producing constant output. Use this space to build a rhythm that honors your energy while still making an impact.

I will not: ....
(e.g., post every day, say yes to every podcast, compare my results to others)

I will pause or delegate: ....
(e.g., social media, administrative tasks, outreach)

- My weekly rhythm looks like
- Send one email every .... weeks.
- Post on ....
- Check in with my community or groups on ....
    - My next rest and recovery date is: ....

What will that pause look like? (Select all you will try)

☐ Celebration (e.g., dinner with friends, meaningful reward)

☐ Quiet reflection (e.g., journaling, meditating, reading)

PROMOTE YOUR PURPOSE

- ☐ Time off (e.g., a full day without book work or responsibilities)
- ☐ Creative play (e.g., painting, music, writing for fun)
- ☐ Movement or nature (e.g., walking, hiking, biking, gardening)
- ☐ Connection (e.g., coffee with a friend, social time, heartfelt conversation)
- ☐ Digital detox (e.g., logging off social media or email for a day)
- ☐ Retreat or staycation (e.g., a no-obligations day or weekend)
- ☐ Sleep or rest day (e.g., nap, sleep in, low-energy activities)
- ☐ Other: ....

Consistency isn't about doing everything. It's about doing what matters most, one step at a time. Keep the conversation alive. Keep showing up. Your words have more power than you know.

Your commitment to promoting your purpose is part of something much bigger than you. The true heart of purpose-driven work is knowing that your influence doesn't end with you but lives on in the people, communities, and movements you touch.

Marketing your book also isn't about staying "on schedule" but about staying in the conversation. Your purpose doesn't expire if you slow down. You're not behind. You're right on time for the impact you're meant to create. Some seasons will be about pushing; others will be about resting and resetting. All are essential. Trust your process. Keep going at the pace your life, your energy, and your mission require.

PUT PURPOSE INTO PRACTICE

Your book's journey is only just beginning. As you nurture its long-term success, ask yourself these questions:

- ✓ What's one simple way I can reconnect with my readers this month?
- ✓ Which existing piece of content could I breathe new life into and share with a new audience?
- ✓ Where can I create a rhythm that feels sustainable, not overwhelming?

CONCLUSION: Your Next Chapter Starts Now

Whether you realize it or not, you didn't just read a book on marketing. You created something bigger by building a purpose-driven path to amplify your message. Every chapter, every exercise, every reflection you completed has been a building block. You now have a foundation strong enough not just to publish your book but to change lives with it, starting with your own. This is not the end of your journey. It's the beginning of everything your book can unlock.

Where You Started

- You began by reconnecting with your purpose and understanding why your book matters, not just for you but for the people who'll read it, share it, and be transformed by it.
- You learned how to think beyond the book itself and build an ecosystem that supports a bigger vision.
- You challenged yourself to think like both an author and a business owner, blending creativity with strategy.
- You confronted the realities of marketing, selling, and sustaining a book, and you didn't back away from the hard parts.

What You Built

- You assessed where you are, where you want to go, and how to get there with clarity and confidence.

PROMOTE YOUR PURPOSE

- You strategized your messaging, your audience, and your goals, aligning them with the heart of your work.
- You mapped a plan that wasn't just about tasks and timelines but also about building momentum that will last.
- You learned to execute with intention, whether you're launching a brand-new book or sustaining its visibility months or even years after release.
- You discovered how to nurture your readers, your marketing ecosystem, and your own energy so that your book stays alive in the hearts and minds of the people it was meant to serve.

Where You're Going Next

The following pages provide you with tools, templates, and an ultimate Book Marketing Essentials Checklist. Along with your skills, you now have a roadmap to keep moving forward, no matter what stage you're in.

- If you're still writing, you know how to build with purpose.
- If you're launching, you know how to create energy and engagement.
- If you've already launched, you know how to nurture ongoing momentum and make your book part of a bigger legacy.

Most importantly, you know that you can do this. Not perfectly, not all at once, but step-by-step. Intentionally. Strategically. Sustainably.

> The most successful authors aren't the ones who do everything perfectly. They're the ones who keep taking action, even when it's imperfect, even when it's messy, even when it feels small.

PROMOTE YOUR PURPOSE

 **TAKE ACTION**
Get Out There and Do It

Every action you take moves your book—and your purpose—closer to the people who need it most. Keep going. You've got this.

Remember: The most successful authors aren't the ones who do everything perfectly. They're the ones who keep taking action, even when it's imperfect, even when it's messy, even when it feels small.

Momentum is built one action at a time. Choose your next step today:

- Send one email.
- Share one insight from your book.
- Follow up with one reader, one influencer, or one community member.

Your readers are waiting. Your impact is waiting. And you already have everything you need to move forward. This was never just about writing a book. It was about making the difference only you can make. Your story is just getting started, and the next chapter begins with you.

PUT PURPOSE INTO PRACTICE

Progress doesn't come from grand gestures. It comes from showing up again and again. Which phase of your ASPEN journey needs your energy today?

- ✓ Assess: What's your next best move?
- ✓ Strategize: How can you align today's actions with your bigger vision?
- ✓ Plan: What step needs structure or momentum behind it?
- ✓ Execute: What small task can you complete right now?
- ✓ Nurture: How will you continue building relationships that carry your work forward?

Choose one, then take action.

EXPAND YOUR PURPOSE

Bring your author goals to life with The Institute for Author Growth and Impact, a self-paced learning platform that helps nonfiction and memoir authors write, publish, and promote their books with clarity and purpose.

Explore programs that help you:

- Build a strong foundation for your manuscript
- Navigate publishing with clarity and confidence
- Promote your book with practical, sustainable strategies

Each program is designed to help you stay focused, take meaningful action, and expand your impact one step at a time.

Explore your next step at
authorgrowthandimpact.org.

APPENDICES

APPENDIX A: Your Book Marketing Essentials Checklist

Take a moment to revisit the core steps you've mapped out through the ASPEN Method. Use this checklist to assess your progress, identify any gaps in your plan, and stay focused, grounded, and confident as you continue to build momentum.

1. **Reconnect with My Purpose, Vision, and Impact (chapter 1)**

   ☐ Do I have a firm understanding of my why?

   ☐ Is my vision aligned with my purpose?

   ☐ Does this align with the impact I want to make?

2. **Set Clear, Strategic Marketing Goals (chapter 2)**

   ☐ Did I identify my top three book promotion goals and turn them into SMART goals?

   ☐ Do I know which goal best fits my current energy, resources, and purpose?

3. **Align My Mindset with My Marketing Goals (chapter 3)**

   ☐ Did I craft a strong tagline and reaffirm my purpose?

   ☐ Did I shift my mindset about marketing and reframe my limiting beliefs?

4. Show Up and Stay Accountable (chapter 4)

- ☐ Did I identify my Strategist, Therapist, and Cheerleader?
- ☐ Did I create "IF this, THEN that" support statements?
- ☐ Did I choose an accountability partner and set a regular check-in rhythm?

5. Map My Author Ecosystem (chapter 5)

- ☐ Did I map how my book connects to my services, speaking, and thought leadership?
- ☐ Do I understand my business model and/or visibility strategies and where my book fits in?
- ☐ Did I identify at least one or two ways I can build meaningful connections and foster engagement so that my book's reach can extend beyond the page?

6. Define My Reader and Buyer (chapter 6)

- ☐ Do I know who my ideal reader is, what problem they face, and the transformation I offer?
- ☐ Do I know who benefits most from reading my book, and who is most likely to buy it?
- ☐ Am I prepared for feedback, both positive and negative?

7. Sell with Purpose (chapter 7)

- ☐ Do I know how I can structure my message and sales in a way that allows me to stay rooted in my values while reaching more people?
- ☐ Am I ready to reframe sales as connections by using the Meet–Invite–Sell framework?

APPENDIX A: YOUR BOOK MARKETING ESSENTIALS CHECKLIST

- ☐ Do I understand where my book fits into my customers' journey?
- ☐ Do I know how I'll invite readers deeper into my work, and do I have a clear plan to stay connected after they say yes?

8. Your Book Marketing Self-Assessment (chapter 8)

- ☐ Do I understand my book's positioning and where I might expand my visibility?
- ☐ Have I leveraged my archived content (e.g., blog posts, webinars, slide decks, etc.)?
- ☐ Did I define three adjectives for my brand and compare them to how others describe me?
- ☐ Do I understand my strengths, weaknesses, opportunities, and threats (SWOT) and how they fit into my marketing strategies?
- ☐ Am I aware of competitor trends, and am I using them to guide my positioning?

9. Define Your CTAs, Partners, and Promotions (chapter 9)

- ☐ Did I choose the next step I want readers to take by drafting at least one strong CTA, and have I determined where to place it?
- ☐ Did I determine whether cause marketing is a fit for my book and, if so, which kind?
- ☐ Did I list two or three potential partners who are aligned with my message or audience?
- ☐ Do I understand my book launch and pre-order strategies?
- ☐ Do I know my publishing status, direct sales opportunities, and bulk sales targets?

10. Create My Book Marketing Roadmap (chapter 10)

- ☐ Did I build my book buyer and influencer lists?
- ☐ Do I know how my influencers will support me?
- ☐ Did I prepare a book review request system?
- ☐ Did I map out my pre-order campaign and bonus tiers?
- ☐ Did I define my marketing boundaries and rhythms?
- ☐ Did I plan a post-launch recovery ritual?

11. From Planning to Executing (chapter 11)

Daily Tasks

- ☐ Have I defined what daily visibility looks like for me?
- ☐ Have I identified the best ways to engage with my audience consistently?
- ☐ Do I have a plan for how and when to review performance data daily?

Weekly Tasks

- ☐ Have I mapped out a realistic weekly content rhythm?
- ☐ Have I identified weekly visibility opportunities?
- ☐ Do I have a system for reviewing and adjusting my strategy each week?
- ☐ Have I built a structure for requesting and following up on reviews?

Monthly Tasks

- ☐ Have I scheduled time each month to review metrics and evaluate what's working?
- ☐ Have I outlined a plan to explore new visibility or promotional opportunities each month?
- ☐ Do I have a system for repurposing content to save time and stay consistent?

APPENDIX A: YOUR BOOK MARKETING ESSENTIALS CHECKLIST

- ☐ Have I built in monthly gratitude practices to acknowledge those supporting my book?
- ☐ Have I decided on my launch type and clarified my launch goals?
- ☐ Have I built pre- and post-launch momentum by identifying one marketing activity I enjoy and committing to making time for it each month?

12. Sustain the Spark (chapter 12)

- ☐ Do I know how I will nurture a steady stream of new reviews after my book's launch?
- ☐ Did I choose a key theme and supporting content to repurpose into new formats?
- ☐ Do I know how I will keep readers engaged and active after they finish my book?
- ☐ Did I strengthen my touchpoints and brainstorm at least one new community space or offering?
- ☐ Did I map three to five steps between "purchase" and "community member"?
- ☐ Did I set clear boundaries around what I won't do?
- ☐ Did I identify tasks to pause or delegate?
- ☐ Did I create a weekly rhythm and choose where I'll show up consistently?
- ☐ Did I schedule my next rest or recovery date and define what that pause looks like?

PROMOTE YOUR PURPOSE

Tally Your Progress

Take a moment to count how many of the previous statements you were able to confidently check off. These aren't just tasks. They are indicators that you've built a strong foundation for your book marketing strategy.

Total items completed: .... of 58

Total items still in progress: .... of 58

If your "still in progress" list feels long, that's okay. This checklist isn't about perfection, it's about awareness. You now have a clear view of where you're strong and where you still have opportunities to grow. Revisit this list anytime you need to re-center, prioritize, or reconnect with your goals.

Remember: Marketing your book is a long game. Keep showing up with purpose, and the impact will follow.

APPENDIX B

TEDx and Signature Talks (Ch. 2)

Publishing a book positions you as a thought leader, and speaking takes that influence to the next level. Whether you're giving a TEDx talk or crafting a signature presentation for conferences, schools, businesses, or virtual events, public speaking can dramatically expand your reach and credibility.

Speaking matters for authors for four main reasons:

1. **Visibility**

   Speaking gives your book exposure to new audiences who may not find it otherwise.

2. **Credibility**

   A well-crafted talk reinforces your authority and makes you a trusted voice in your field.

3. **Sales and Leads**

   Audiences often want more after a great talk, and your book is the natural next step.

4. **Mission Amplification**

   A stage helps you advocate for your message in a powerful, lasting way.

PROMOTE YOUR PURPOSE

What Is a TEDx Talk?

TEDx is a locally organized, independently run version of the TED platform. TEDx talks must follow TED's format: under 18 minutes, focused on "an idea worth spreading," and non-promotional in nature. TEDx is ideal for authors with a bold idea that can stand alone from their book but is still deeply connected to it. A TEDx talk can serve as a powerful entry point to your larger body of work as well as build demand for your book organically.

Many events are curated, and organizers seek compelling, credible voices, so there are two key guidelines here:

1. No selling from the stage (your book can be mentioned only subtly or in your bio).
2. Content must be educational, insightful, or paradigm-shifting.

Use this worksheet to prepare your concept and application materials so that you're prepared to apply with confidence and clarity.

1. What Is Your "Idea Worth Spreading"?

This should stand alone from your book's promotion but can still relate to it.

My core TEDx idea is: ....

....

....

....

It's original because: ....

....

....

....

APPENDIX B: TEDX AND SIGNATURE TALKS (CH. 2)

It challenges or reframes the way people think about: ....

....

....

....

2. Talk Summary (two or three sentences)

This may go directly into your TEDx application.

Summary: ....

....

....

....

3. How Your Book Supports the Talk

TEDx organizers may look you up. Be prepared to show alignment without sounding promotional.

My book supports the idea by: ....

....

....

....

Readers who liked the talk would get even more value from: ....

....

....

....

PROMOTE YOUR PURPOSE

4. TEDx Event Search Plan

Visit ted.com/tedx and identify a few events you could apply to.

Local TEDx events to explore: ....

....

....

....

Application deadline(s): ....

Contact person or link: ....

What Is a Signature Talk?

Similar to TEDx, a signature talk is a repeatable presentation built around your core message. It can evolve over time and be adapted to different audiences or industries, but the essence stays the same. Think of it as the live expression of your book's mission.

A great signature talk does four things:

1. Tells a compelling personal or client story
2. Highlights key lessons or takeaways from your book
3. Moves the audience to reflect, act, or explore more
4. Ends with a clear next step (which could include buying your book, joining your list, or booking a follow-up conversation)

Use this worksheet to develop a talk that amplifies your purpose and grows your platform.

1. Your Core Message

What is the big idea or transformation your talk delivers?

My core message is: ....

....

APPENDIX B: TEDX AND SIGNATURE TALKS (CH. 2)

2. Your Foundational Story

Choose a personal story, client example, or lived experience that illustrates your message.

The story I'll share is about: ....

....

....

....

It connects to my book because: ....

....

....

....

The key takeaway is: ....

....

....

....

3. Supporting Points or Lessons

What ideas, tools, or chapters from your book support your message?

....

....

....

....

4. CTAs

What do you want the audience to do after your talk? (Check all that apply)

- ☐ Buy your book
- ☐ Download a resource
- ☐ Book you to speak or consult
- ☐ Reflect or take a personal action
- ☐ Other: ....

My closing line or CTA will be: ....
....
....
....

5. Format and Timing

This talk can be adapted for (Check all that apply):

- ☐ Keynote
- ☐ Panel
- ☐ Webinar
- ☐ Workshop
- ☐ Podcast

Ideal length: .... minutes.

Idea-Generating Questions

Use these prompts if you're just beginning to shape your talk or want to spark new ideas:

What's one core message from your book you want to be known for?

....
....
....
....
....

What story (yours or someone else's) illustrates that message powerfully?

....
....
....
....
....

What's the transformation or aha moment you want your audience to experience?

....
....
....
....
....

PROMOTE YOUR PURPOSE

How can your book offer a next step after the talk?

....

....

....

....

....

Calls to Action Examples (Ch. 10)

APPENDIX C

Use the following examples to craft CTAs that guide your reader toward deeper engagement. Choose one or more based on your goals, whether you're building your email list, booking speaking gigs, or driving bulk sales.

Grow Your Email List

- Get free access to my resource library at [yourwebsite.com].
- Want a sneak peek? Download the first chapter free and start your journey today.
- Join my newsletter for weekly insights, behind-the-scenes updates, and tools to support your growth.

Book Speaking or Consulting Opportunities

- Interested in bringing this message to your organization? Let's talk.
- Book me to speak at your next event, workshop, or team retreat.
- Looking for a thought partner or adviser? Reach out for a consultation.

Drive Book Sales and Pre-Orders

- Buy your copy today and start the conversation that matters.
- Pre-order now to receive exclusive bonuses and early access.
- Order in bulk for your team or classroom. Special rates are available.

Promote Additional Resources or Products

- Explore the workbook, templates, and companion tools at [yourwebsite.com].
- Want help putting this into practice? Check out [XYZ].
- Grab the companion workbook for guided exercises and implementation support.

Invite Conversations and Community

- Tell me how this book landed for you, tag me on social, or send me a note.
- Join our community of changemakers at [Private Group / Social Media / Slack link].
- Let's keep the conversation going! Share your biggest takeaway from this chapter.

Incentivize with Bonuses

- Send proof of purchase to [email] and receive our exclusive bonus guide.
- Get our [XYZ] free when you order two or more copies.
- Bonus content awaits. Visit [link] after you order your book.

Pre-order Examples

Pre-orders are a powerful way to spark momentum, build community, and reward your earliest supporters. Here are real and inspired CTAs organized by type of bonus or audience strategy. Use these ideas to customize your own pre-order campaign.

Bonuses Content

- Pre-order today and receive exclusive bonus materials not included in the book.

- Order early and get access to a downloadable resource designed to help you apply what you've read.
- As a thank-you for your early support, you'll receive a behind-the-scenes look at how the book was created.

Companion Tools and Downloads

- Pre-order and unlock a printable worksheet, checklist, or action guide to support your learning.
- Get access to a companion workbook sample when you place your pre-order.
- Early buyers will receive a planning tool that aligns with a key chapter in the book.

Speaker/Workshop-Driven Offers

- Order three or more copies and you'll get access to my recorded signature talk that expands on the book's message.
- Pre-order 10 copies and I'll join your team call or book club for a live Q&A session.
- Bulk pre-orders come with a custom workshop based on your organization's goals. Email for details.

Audience-Specific CTAs (for Coaches, Consultants, and Memoirists)

- Pre-order to receive a guide on how to use your book as a client onboarding tool.
- If you're using your book to grow a speaking business, this bonus training is for you! Pre-order now.
- Memoir writers: Pre-order and get a bonus worksheet on how to share your story without retraumatizing yourself.

Thought Leadership and Long-Term Strategy

- Pre-order to receive a strategic guide that builds on the book's teachings.
- Get early access to an upcoming course or toolset inspired by the book.
- Supporters who pre-order will receive an exclusive case study tied to the book's message.

Community Access

- Pre-order and get an invite to a private Q&A session or live author event.
- Join our reader community and participate in a special pre-launch discussion group.
- Early supporters get access to an exclusive webinar or virtual book club session.

Engagement-Driven Offers

- Pre-order and your name will be featured in my launch thank-you post.
- Share your receipt and why you're excited about this book, and you could win a 1:1 strategy session.
- First 25 pre-orders get a handwritten note and a signed bookmark to say thank you for believing in this mission.

For Academic or Organizational Use

- Ideal for educators, team leaders, or facilitators, email to learn more about classroom or training bonuses.
- Pre-order for your team or school and receive a group reading guide or institutional discount.
- Special offers are available for libraries, colleges, or nonprofit partners. Bulk inquiries welcome.

APPENDIX D
Key Ad Metrics for Paid Campaigns (Ch. 11)

Paid ads can help increase visibility, drive book sales, and grow your audience—but only if you monitor their performance and adjust as needed. Tracking your metrics helps ensure your money is well spent. Here's a breakdown of what this means and why it's important:

METRIC	WHAT IT MEANS	WHY IT'S IMPORTANT
Impressions	The number of times your ad is shown	Helps you gauge reach and visibility
Clicks	How many people click on your ad	High click numbers suggest your messaging and targeting are compelling
Cost Per Click (CPC)	The average cost for each click	Helps you assess the efficiency of your ad spend
Conversion Rate	The percentage of people who take the desired action	Shows how well your ads and landing pages are working
Ad Spend	Total money spent on a campaign	Helps you stay within budget
Cost of Sales	How much advertising costs	Shows how much you're spending to make a sale
Return on Ad Spend (ROAS)	Revenue earned equals money spent	Help you evaluate your overall profitability

PROMOTE YOUR PURPOSE

Use this table to track your weekly ad performance across platforms. This will help you monitor trends and make informed, data-driven decisions.

DATE	PLATFORM	IMPRESSIONS	CLICKS	CPC	CONVERSION	AD SPEND	ROAS
Week 1							
Week 2							
Week 3							
Week 4							

Even with a small ad budget, it's important to monitor what's working and what isn't. Watch for common patterns that can help you identify when to make strategic adjustments before wasting time or money:

> To access a downloadable spreadsheet for tracking your metrics, visit: **promoteyourpurpose book.com/bonuses.**

- ▸ Are you getting clicks but no conversions? Adjust your landing page or offer.
- ▸ Are your costs high but sales low? Revisit your target audience or ad copy.
- ▸ Is one platform outperforming the rest? Shift your budget toward what's working.

APPENDIX D: KEY AD METRICS FOR PAID CAMPAIGNS (CH. 11)

Tracking your ads doesn't have to be time-consuming or complicated. Here are some ways to stay focused, make informed decisions, and stretch your marketing dollars further:

- Set a weekly time block to review your ad metrics.
- Use A/B testing: Run two ads with slight variations to see which performs best.
- Track organic versus paid impact to make informed decisions over time.
- If this isn't your wheelhouse, consider outsourcing this to an expert.

APPENDIX E
Marketing to Academic Institutions (Ch. 11)

If your book has the potential to be used as a teaching tool or to influence a field of study, academic institutions can be a powerful audience. While this path takes time, effort, and patience, the long-term rewards can include consistent book sales, increased credibility, and lasting impact on students and professionals alike.

Is Academic Marketing Right for You?

Before diving into this strategy, ask yourself:

- Is your book nonfiction or a memoir with clear learning objectives?
- Was your book designed to teach, inform, or present a framework or methodology?
- Are comparable books currently being used in academic programs?
- Can your content be integrated into a syllabus as required or supplemental reading?

Even if your book wasn't written with academia in mind, many authors discover opportunities after publication by positioning their books around key topics being taught in degree or certificate programs.

Benefits of Academic Outreach

The benefits of academic outreach can be both immediate and long-lasting. Once your book is adopted into a course, it can generate sustained sales as it is reordered semester after semester. Beyond sales, your content has the potential to shape early-career thinking, helping students form perspectives on your topic before they enter the workforce. Engaging with academic institutions can also elevate your visibility as a thought leader, as professors, department heads, and program directors often become valuable allies in amplifying your message. Additionally, this kind of exposure can lead to referrals and open doors to speaking, consulting, and other collaborative opportunities.

Finding the Right Institutions

Start by identifying institutions that align with your topic. Consider:

- Colleges, universities, and community colleges
- Certificate and continuing education programs
- Vocational schools or training institutes
- High school enrichment or transition programs

Focus on programs related to your book's themes. If you wrote about workplace culture, HR, or leadership, look into business schools, executive education programs, or professional development departments. Also consider geographic relevance, alma maters, or institutions where you have existing relationships.

Who to Contact

Each institution is different, but possible contacts include:

- Adjunct or full-time professors
- Program chairs or department heads
- Deans or academic affairs staff
- Course designers or curriculum committees

Start with professors, especially adjuncts, since they often have greater flexibility in choosing course materials.

APPENDIX E: MARKETING TO ACADEMIC INSTITUTIONS (CH. 11)

Outreach Strategy

Decide how many institutions you want to contact each month and what you plan to send. Your outreach may include:

- A personal email or letter of introduction
- A digital version of your book or sample chapters
- A sample syllabus outlining how your book fits into their curriculum
- A discussion guide with reflection or group questions
- An offer to send a complimentary desk copy for review

Customize each outreach with a clear explanation of how your book supports the program's learning goals. The easier you make it for instructors to visualize using your book, the better.

Timing and Follow-Up

Academic institutions plan syllabi months in advance. Fall courses are often planned in the spring, and spring courses are often planned in the fall. When in doubt, assume at least a six-month lead time.

Track your efforts in a spreadsheet, including names, titles, dates of outreach, responses, and follow-up timelines. Stay organized, and know that it's common not to hear back until months later.

To stay organized and on track, download our Academic Outreach Tracker at **promoteyourpurposebook.com/bonuses.** Use it to log contacts, follow-up dates, and responses so you can manage your outreach without missing a beat.

Incentivize the Decision

Make it easy for faculty to say yes by offering one or more of the following bonuses:

- A sample syllabus that shows exactly where and how your book fits into a course
- Chapter-by-chapter discussion questions
- A guest lecture (in-person or virtual)
- Companion resources such as a workbook or handouts

These extras demonstrate that your book isn't just content but is designed for the classroom.

Final Thought

Academic marketing is a long game, but the payoff can be deeply rewarding. When your book becomes part of a learning experience, you're not just selling copies, you're shaping minds.

This approach works best when aligned with your broader strategy of purpose-driven visibility. It requires intention, organization, and relationship-building, but it has the power to create lasting impact beyond what you might achieve through traditional book marketing channels alone.

If you're not sure where to begin, choose three programs or schools that you feel excited to explore. Reach out. Offer value. Track your responses. Repeat. The effort you invest today could pay off for years to come.

APPENDIX F

Your On-the-Go Author Kit (Ch. 11)

Whether you're attending a book festival, setting up at a farmers' market, or speaking at a corporate event, having an On-the-Go Author Kit ensures you'll be prepared, professional, and ready to make the most of the opportunity. Use this checklist to pack efficiently and avoid last-minute scrambles.

Essentials for Selling or Signing Books

- [ ] Copies of your book (bring more than you think you'll need; you'll get a sense after a few times, but for distant conferences start with no more than 20 copies, accept payment on-site, and ship signed books later to avoid attendees carrying heavy copies home)
- [ ] Table, tablecloth, and signage (banner or standing sign)
- [ ] Bookstands or easels to display books upright
- [ ] Pens or markers for signing
- [ ] Bookmark or flyer with QR code to your website or social media
- [ ] Business cards
- [ ] Cash box (with cash to make change), credit card reader, and QR code payment options
- [ ] Receipt book or digital transaction tracker
- [ ] Sales tax information (check your state-specific laws)

PROMOTE YOUR PURPOSE

Marketing and Visibility Tools

- [ ] Branded table runner or pop-up banner
- [ ] Email sign-up sheet or tablet with digital form
- [ ] Small giveaway or raffle (optional, but increases engagement)
- [ ] Testimonial cards or media mentions on display
- [ ] Social media handles clearly visible
- [ ] Small framed signage (e.g., "Author book signing here!" or "Book a speaking event")

Comfort and Practical Items

- [ ] Water bottle and snacks
- [ ] Sunscreen, a hat, or a portable fan (for outdoor events)
- [ ] Extra layers (if indoors and air conditioned)
- [ ] Portable phone charger
- [ ] Notepad for tracking contacts, questions, or ideas
- [ ] Tape, scissors, zip ties, or binder clips (for signage emergencies)
- [ ] Multi-tool (pliers, scissors, screwdriver; perfect for quick fixes)

Bonus Prep Tips

- [ ] Do a quick mock setup at home to visualize your table.
- [ ] Practice your short pitch so you feel confident when people stop by.
- [ ] Have a small mirror on hand (you'll thank yourself).
- [ ] Pack everything in a rolling suitcase or utility cart for easy transport.

APPENDIX G

Book Launch Email Examples (Ch. 11)

Your launch day email doesn't need to be fancy, it just needs to be clear, personal, and easy to act on. This appendix offers three styles of launch announcement emails you can adapt depending on your tone and goals. Each includes a strong subject line, concise body copy, and a clear call to action.

Before you write, decide what tone feels most aligned with your brand and audience, whether it's professional, conversational, or celebratory, and determine whether you want to include emojis or keep the formatting clean and simple.

For a copy and paste version of these email examples, please visit **promoteyourpurposebook.com/bonuses**.

Example 1: Personal and Heartfelt

Subject: It's here! My book is officially available!

Hi [Subscriber first name],

I can't believe this day is finally here. After months (okay, years) of writing, editing, and dreaming, my book [*Book Title*] is officially available for purchase!

This book is deeply personal to me. It's about [*insert quick summary of what the book helps with or why it matters*]. Whether you're new to my work or have followed this journey from the beginning, I'm so grateful to have you in my corner.

PROMOTE YOUR PURPOSE

You can order your copy here: [*Insert purchase link*]

If you've ever thought, *I should write a book,* or if you're trying to [*insert desired outcome for the reader*], I wrote this for you.

Thank you for supporting me, sharing the message, and helping me get this book into the hands of those who need it most.

With gratitude,

[Your Name]

[Optional PS: A request for Amazon reviews or social shares]

Example 2: Direct and Professional

Subject: My new book is now available—get your copy today!

Hi [Subscriber first name],

I'm excited to share that my book [*Book Title*] is officially live and available for purchase!

This book was created to help [*ideal reader*] learn how to [*problem the book solves or transformation it offers*]. It's packed with real stories, practical tools, and actionable strategies to help readers [*key outcome*].

Get your copy now: [*Insert purchase link*]

If you find the book valuable, I'd love it if you'd leave a quick Amazon review or forward this email to someone who might benefit.

Thanks for being part of this journey.

Warmly,

[Your Name]

[Some optional items to consider are an author bio, a press/media link, or or a call to action to join a launch event.]

Example 3: High-Energy and Promotional

Subject: It's launch day! Special bonus inside

Hey [Subscriber first name],

It's finally here! My new book [*Book Title*] is officially out in the world, and I've got something special for you.

Today only! If you grab a copy and forward your receipt to [*your email*], I'll send you [insert bonus—e.g., workbook, exclusive video, resource guide].

Buy the book here: [*Insert link*]

Whether you're looking to [*key benefit*] or just love learning through real-world stories, this book is for you.

Thanks for cheering me on. Today's the day!

Let's do this,

[Your Name]

[Optional PS: "After you read, I'd love your honest review on Amazon—it makes a huge difference."]

Before You Hit "Send"

As you sit down to write your launch email, remember to keep it simple and focused. A clear subject line goes a long way, so don't be afraid to lead with the announcement that your book is available. You've worked hard to reach this milestone, and your audience wants to hear about it. Here are a few other things to think about:

- Visuals can help your message stand out, so consider adding your book cover to the body of your email. It's a great way to create a visual connection with your readers, and it adds a sense of legitimacy and excitement.

PROMOTE YOUR PURPOSE

- Emojis can boost visibility and convey tone quickly, especially in subject lines. A well-placed emoji can make your message feel warm, energetic, or timely, but too many can feel gimmicky or unprofessional. If your brand voice is upbeat and informal, a celebratory emoji might fit well, but if you're writing to a more formal or corporate audience, skip it.

- Try not to overwhelm your audience with too many links. One or two clear CTAs, ideally to the same sales page, are more effective than giving people too many options. Make it easy for them to say yes.

- Remember that not everyone will see your email the first time. It's completely normal (and encouraged) to send a follow-up email 24–48 hours later to people who didn't open the original. A quick reminder can help you stay top-of-mind without being pushy.

Ultimately, your launch email is just one moment in your larger marketing journey. Let it reflect who you are, celebrate this accomplishment, and invite your audience to join you for what comes next.

TAKE ACTION BEYOND THE PAGE

Bring the ASPEN Method to life with the Promote Your Purpose Action Deck, a set of 48 cards designed to keep your marketing momentum going long after you close this book.

Each card features a practical, purpose-driven prompt drawn from the five phases of the ASPEN Method.

Use the deck to:

- Spark new marketing ideas when you feel stuck
- Stay consistent with small, actionable steps each week
- Inspire reflection and alignment with your bigger mission

Whether you pull one card a week or use them to guide a focused sprint, the deck helps you turn insight into impact one action at a time.

Get your deck at
promoteyourpurposebook.com/deck.

READER RESOURCES

You've laid the foundation, and you've launched or are preparing to launch, and now the real work begins: keeping your book visible, impactful, and growing.

Marketing isn't a one-time event; it's an ongoing journey. The following tools, programs, and resources are here to support you at every stage, whether you're still writing, actively launching, or sustaining long-term momentum.

Marketing Support

Your book is a platform, not just a product. With the right strategy, it can expand your visibility, attract aligned opportunities, and deepen your impact over time. From launch planning to content repurposing and long-term outreach, we provide guidance and resources to help your message reach the right people. Not everything could fit in this book, so this is where you'll find fresh strategies, real author examples, and honest guidance that can be delivered to your inbox.

- Access free templates, case studies, and strategic tools at promoteyourpurposebook.com/bonuses.
- Keep your marketing momentum going with the Promote Your Purpose Action Deck, featuring 48 prompts to help you apply the ASPEN Method—available at promoteyourpurposebook.com/card-deck
- Subscribe to my Substack for book marketing insights at promoteyourpurpose.substack.com.

Publishing Support

When you're ready to publish, we're here to guide you through the process with clarity and integrity. As a hybrid publisher, PYP partners with purpose-driven authors to produce high-quality nonfiction books and memoirs that make a difference. Submit your manuscript through our Publish With Us application and take the next step toward working with PYP at publishyourpurpose.com/publishing-support.

Writing Support

If you're still working on your manuscript, your priority is to build momentum and finish strong. From idea to draft, we support authors at all stages of the writing process through a range of free and paid services that offer structure, accountability, and community. Explore available writing support at publishyourpurpose.com/writing-support.

ACKNOWLEDGMENTS

Every book is built on more than words. It's built on community, collaboration, and the quiet (and not-so-quiet) encouragement of those who believe in what you're trying to create.

To the incredible PYP authors who graciously shared early feedback and reflections on this manuscript—Michelle Bogan, Chris Chavis, Sam Cherubin, Jennifer Hayden, Kim Hermberg, Hady Mendez, Frank Miles, David T. Norman, Christiane Scarpino, and Deborah D. Vereen—thank you. Your willingness to engage with this work while it was still in progress means more than you know. This book is stronger because of your insight and generosity and the depth of your perspective.

To my thought partners and truth-tellers, Alyssa Berthiaume, Jennifer Brown, Allison Davis, Nell Derick Debevoise, Tina Dietz, N. Chloé Nwangwu, Eduardo Placer, Bernadette Smith, and Steve Yacovelli, thank you for continually expanding how I think about leadership, purpose, and voice. Your presence in my world makes everything I create sharper, deeper, and more aligned.

To Niki Garcia, our chief operating officer and my constant sounding board since PYP was just an idea back in 2015, thank you. You are the steady force behind the scenes who keeps this company grounded, focused, and thriving. None of this would be possible without you.

To the rest of the incredible team behind the scenes at PYP, thank you for the time, space, structure, and spirit you brought to this project. I'm especially grateful to Alexander Loutsenko, Catherine Whiting, Brandi Lai, and Vikki Brown for your steady support and attention to detail at every turn.

To Nancy Graham-Tillman and Lily Capstick, thank you for your thoughtful editing support. Your attention, insight, and care helped bring clarity and refinement to these pages.

To Nelly Murariu and Mark Pate for your brilliant vision and execution of both the inside and outside design of this book.

PROMOTE YOUR PURPOSE

To my family, thank you for allowing me to borrow time from our precious moments together to bring this book into the world. Your love and support are the foundation of everything I do.

This book is the result of more than a decade of experience in publishing and over two decades in marketing, and it reflects countless conversations, lessons, and iterations along the way. To everyone who has challenged me to grow, offered encouragement at the right moment, or shown up with heart, I see you in these pages.

And to you, the reader, thank you for trusting me to be part of your journey. Your purpose matters. Your voice matters. The world needs the story only you can tell. Keep going. You're making a bigger difference than you realize.

ABOUT JENN

An award-winning author, nationally recognized speaker, and publishing strategist, Jenn T. Grace has built her career at the intersection of marketing, communication, and storytelling. Before founding her acclaimed hybrid publishing company, Publish Your Purpose, Jenn spent over two decades helping businesses succeed, starting in her early 20s when she launched a marketing firm that created websites and print materials for local entrepreneurs. She later ran a consulting practice focused on internal communications and external marketing strategies for corporate and nonprofit clients.

Today, Jenn brings that marketing expertise to the heart of everything at Publish Your Purpose, a certified B Corp social enterprise dedicated to helping purpose-driven authors not just write and publish their books but strategically market them for long-term success. Jenn believes a book should be more than a product; it should be a catalyst for impact, visibility, and growth.

A 20+ year veteran of the marketing world, Jenn went on to earn a master's degree in integrated marketing communications, giving her a unique ability to bridge creative storytelling with smart business strategy. She has guided over 300 first-time authors through writing, publishing, and launching books that align with their larger goals, whether growing a business, expanding a platform, or sparking a movement.

Jenn is the author of eight books, including *Publish Your Purpose: A Step-By-Step Guide to Write, Publish, and Grow Your Big Idea* and her memoir, *House on Fire: Finding Resilience, Hope, and Purpose in the Ashes*. She has been recognized with multiple "40 Under 40" awards for her leadership and entrepreneurial achievements, and her work has been featured in major media outlets, including *Forbes*, the *Huffington Post*, *The Wall Street Journal*, and CNBC.

PROMOTE YOUR PURPOSE

OTHER BOOKS BY THE AUTHOR

Jenn T. Grace is the author of eight books, including *Publish Your Purpose* and *House on Fire*, with more titles planned for the future. You can explore all of her books at publishyourpurpose.com/authors/jenn-t-grace.

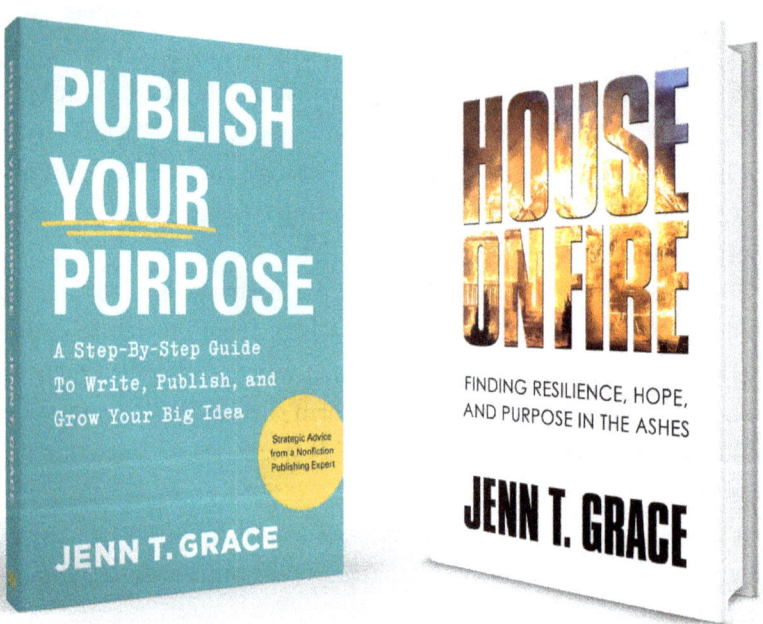

HIRE JENN TO SPEAK

Bring purpose, strategy, and inspiration to your next event with Jenn T. Grace as your speaker.

A nationally recognized speaker, award-winning author, and publishing strategist, Jenn brings over 20 years of marketing and communications experience to every stage she steps on. She blends marketing expertise, storytelling mastery, and real-world business strategies and insights to create engaging and unforgettable audience experiences across industries. Her keynote topics include publishing strategy, building an authentic thought leadership platform, leading with empathy, conscious entrepreneurship, and the power of inclusive storytelling.

Known for her honest, approachable style and her ability to make even complex ideas feel accessible, Jenn has captivated audiences ranging from entrepreneurs and corporate executives to nonprofit leaders and educators. Whether your event is focused on business growth, marketing, or thought leadership, Jenn delivers content that resonates and moves people to act.

To inquire about bringing Jenn to your next event, visit publishyourpurpose.com/contact.

PROMOTE YOUR PURPOSE

THE B CORP MOVEMENT

Dear Reader,

Thank you for reading this book and for joining the Publish Your Purpose community! You are joining a special group of people who aim to make the world a better place.

What's Publish Your Purpose About?

Our mission is to elevate the voices often excluded from traditional publishing. We intentionally seek out authors and storytellers with diverse backgrounds, life experiences, and unique perspectives to publish books that will make an impact in the world.

Beyond our books, we are focused on tangible, action-based change. As a woman- and LGBTQ+-owned company, we are committed to reducing inequality, lowering levels of poverty, creating a healthier environment, building stronger communities, and creating high-quality jobs with dignity and purpose.

As a Certified B Corporation, we use business as a force for good. We join a community of mission-driven companies building a more equitable, inclusive, and sustainable global economy. B Corporations must meet high standards of transparency, social and environmental performance, and accountability as determined by the nonprofit B Lab. The certification process is rigorous and ongoing (with a recertification requirement every three years).

How Do We Do This?

We intentionally partner with socially and economically disadvantaged businesses that meet our sustainability goals. We embrace and encourage our authors and employee's differences in race, age, color, disability, ethnicity, family or marital status, gender identity or expression, language, national origin, physical and mental ability, political affiliation, religion, sexual orientation, socioeconomic status, veteran status, and other characteristics that make them unique.

Community is at the heart of everything we do—from our writing and publishing programs to contributing to social enterprise nonprofits, including reSET (resetco.org) and our work in founding B Local Connecticut.

We are endlessly grateful to our authors, readers, and local community for being the driving force behind the equitable and sustainable world we're building together.

To connect with us online or to publish with us, visit us at publishyourpurpose.com.

Elevating Your Voice,

Jenn T Grace

Jenn T. Grace
Founder, Publish Your Purpose

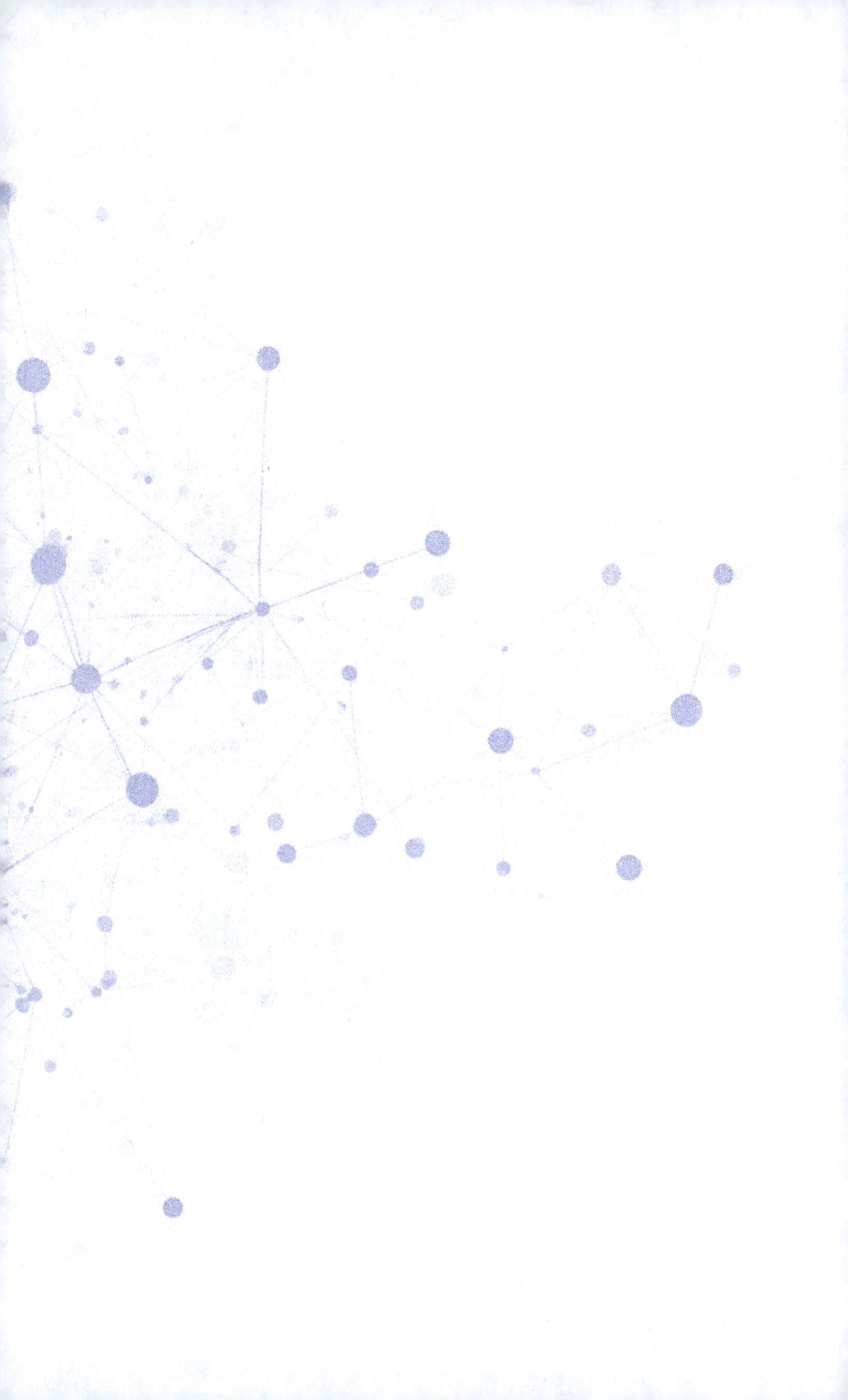

www.ingramcontent.com/pod-product-compliance
Lightning Source LLC
Chambersburg PA
CBHW070719160426
43192CB00009B/1249